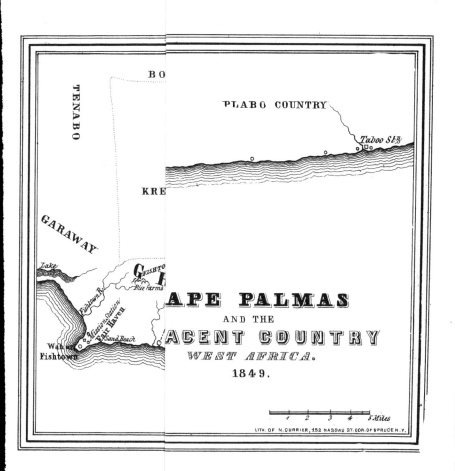

TENABO

BO

PLABO COUNTRY

Taboo St⅞

KRE

GARAWAY

Lake

GEISHTO

Rice farms

Fishtown B.

Mission Station

Fair Haven

Sand Beach

Wah and
Fishtown

APE PALMAS

AND THE

ACENT COUNTRY

WEST AFRICA.

1849.

1 2 3 4 5 Miles

LITH. OF N. CURRIER, 152 NASSAU ST. COR. OF SPRUCE N.Y.

HISTORY OF THE AFRICAN MISSION
OF THE
PROTESTANT EPISCOPAL CHURCH

HISTORY OF THE AFRICAN MISSION
OF THE
PROTESTANT EPISCOPAL CHURCH

By

Mrs. E. F. Hening

The Black Heritage Library Collection

BOOKS FOR LIBRARIES PRESS
FREEPORT, NEW YORK
1971

First Published 1849
Reprinted 1971

Reprinted from a copy in the
Fisk University Library Negro Collection

INTERNATIONAL STANDARD BOOK NUMBER:
0-8369-8900-7

LIBRARY OF CONGRESS CATALOG CARD NUMBER:
77-173608

PRINTED IN THE UNITED STATES OF AMERICA
BY
NEW WORLD BOOK MANUFACTURING CO., INC.
HALLANDALE, FLORIDA 33009

HISTORY

OF THE

AFRICAN MISSION

OF THE

PROTESTANT EPISCOPAL CHURCH

IN THE UNITED STATES,

WITH

MEMOIRS OF DECEASED MISSIONARIES,

AND

NOTICES OF NATIVE CUSTOMS.

BY

MRS. E. F. HENING.

NEW-YORK:

STANFORD AND SWORDS, 137, BROADWAY.

1850.

PREFACE.

THE object of the writer in compiling this little
volume, has been, to present in one view, the
leading historical facts of the Mission of the Protestant Episcopal Church in Western Africa, with
the Memoirs of those who have died in its service,
and such information respecting the country and
customs of the people, as might be interesting to
the general reader. Most of the details have been
collated from the journals of the missionaries,
published in the " Spirit of Missions ;" and if the
work be useful only in directing attention to that
interesting and important periodical, it will not
have been written in vain. That the Members of
the Church are not, generally, as familiar with its

pages as might be expected, has been proved to the writer, by the numerous inquiries which have been addressed to her during her present visit to the United States, and which she has endeavored to answer in this work.

It may serve also to refresh the memories of those who, having been once familiar with the scenes here described, have partially forgotten them ; or, addressing itself to another large class of readers, may convey information of what was done in Africa, either before they were old enough or wise enough to be interested in the work of Missions. For such information, they can hardly be expected to search through the old volumes of a periodical, while they will gladly avail themselves of the labors of another, who offers it for their perusal in a more convenient form.

For the materials for one of the most interesting portions of the volume, the writer is chiefly indebted to the Rev. E. W. Syle, who designed to prepare the Memoir of the lamented Minor for publication, in a separate form, but was unable to complete the work before he sailed for China.

Such as it is, the volume is now sent forth to claim the notice of a leisure hour from all who feel an interest in the extension of the Redeemer's kingdom. May God make it instrumental in deepening that interest, and prompting to more fervent prayer and liberal effort, not only for Africa, but for all the nations who now " sit in darkness."

E. F. H.

BROOKLYN, N. Y., *November*, 1849.

TABLE OF CONTENTS.

CHAPTER I.

CHAPTER II.

CHAPTER III.

CHAPTER IV.

CHAPTER V.

CHAPTER VI.

CHAPTER VII.

CHAPTER VIII.

CHAPTER IX.

CHAPTER X.

CHAPTER XI.

CHAPTER XII.

CHAPTER XIII.

CHAPTER XIV.

CHAPTER XV.

CHAPTER XVI.

CHAPTER XVII.

CHAPTER XVIII.

CHAPTER XIX.

CHAPTER XX.

CHAPTER XXI.

CHAPTER XXII.

CHAPTER XXIII.

CHAPTER XXIV.

CHAPTER XXV.

CHAPTER XXXIII.

CHAPTER XXXIV.

CHAPTER XXXV.

HISTORY

OF

THE AFRICAN MISSION.

CHAPTER. I.

Origin of first Missionary efforts of the Protestant Episcopal Church in the
United States—First Agents of Colonial Society—Appointment of Mr.
Ephraim Bacon—Mr. Jacob Oson -Mission School at Hartford—Mr. James
Thompson—Donation from American Colonial Society—Selection of Mount
Vaughan as a Missionary Station

WE trace the origin of the first missionary organization
of the Protestant Episcopal Church in the United States,
to an impulse received from the mother Church of
England.* In 1815, the Rev. Josiah Pratt, Secretary
of the Church Missionary Society, London, addressed
a circular letter to several of the leading members of the
Episcopal body in this country, in the hope of obtaining
their co-operation in the work of Missions. To this
circular, the late lamented Bishop Griswold was the
first to respond ; and with his reply, he transmitted
to Mr. Pratt a pastoral letter, addressed to his clergy
in 1814, in which he uses the following language :
"Some efforts have been made, and are still in

* See Rev. Dr. Stone's Memoir of Bishop Griswold.

agitation, by a few individuals, to form Missionary Societies, and to collect a little fund for sending the light and comforts of the gospel among those who are destitute. We are far from believing that there is any repugnance to this good work among Christians of our communion : yet from some unhappy cause, it is but too evident that your serious attention has not been duly engaged in this important subject. * * *

"Our numbers are few, and thinly scattered over a large extent of country ; nor have we, until very lately, been so organized and united, as to attempt, with any probability of success, any missionary labors. But now, through divine goodness, these obstacles are in part removed ; our Churches flourish ; our numbers increase ; and we may conveniently unite in any measures to promote the cause of Christianity."

Bishop Griswold assures Mr. Pratt of the cordial co-operation of the American Church, so far as her "means and power will admit." "Most gladly would we unite with you," he writes, "in sending missionaries to Africa and the East ; and hope that the time is not far distant when some of our pious young men will be zealously disposed to engage in this good work. At present, however, we have not the funds, nor other means of doing much in missionary labor ; not even of supplying the wants of our own country."

In a subsequent communication, he introduces to the notice of the Church Missionary Society, the Rev. Joseph R. Andrus, as one anxious to be employed in the missionary field.

The report of the Society for 1817, presents the

following statement :—" the Committee *have suggested*
the expediency of forming in the Episcopal Church of
the United States, a Missionary Society for the ad-
vancement of the kingdom of Christ among the
heathen; and have authorized Bishop Griswold to draw
on this Society for the sum of £200, as an encouragement to its own exertions, and in full persuasion that
those exertions will be, as they are daily found to be in
this country, a blessing to those who make them, as
well as to those towards whose immediate benefit they
are directed. The Committee have also suggested the
propriety of the Rev. Mr. Andrus, before mentioned,
proceeding to Ceylon, under the patronage of the Society
to be so formed ; in the hope, that the maintenance by
the Institution of a pious and exemplary layman among
the heathen, will not only call forth the liberal contri-
butions of the members of the American Episcopal
Church in support of the funds, but excite their prayers
for its success, and induce other clergymen to follow his
example."

Although, as a body, the Church had been too long
negligent of her obligations to the heathen world, it
cannot be doubted that the missionary flame burned
brightly in many hearts within her communion. There
were some, among both her clergy and laity, fully imbued
with the missionary spirit, and willing to encounter any
dangers, and submit to any trials, if they might be the
instruments of good to the perishing heathen. While
the Church remained destitute of any Society under
whose auspices they might go forth on their errand of
love, it was natural that such spirits should embrace

with ardor, the opportunity afforded by the project of
African Colonization, of carrying the gospel to one of
the darkest corners of the globe. We rejoice to find
clergymen of the Protestant Episcopal Church among
the first agents in that noble enterprise.

Such were the Rev. Samuel Bacon, Christian Wilt-
berger, Joseph R. Andrus, and Jehudi Ashmun; and
John P. Bankson, and Ephraim Bacon, were also lay
members of her communion. As, however, the labors
of these gentlemen were unconnected with the missionary efforts of our Church in that country, they are
not included within the limits of this work. Most of
them fell early victims to the pestilential climate of
Africa; and their brief career is appropriately mentioned
in Dr. Alexander's very interesting "History of African
Colonization."

The Domestic and Foreign Missionary Society of
the Protestant Episcopal Church in the United States,
was formed by the General Convention in May, 1820.
The attention of the Society was early turned towards
the destitute millions of Africa, among whom they were
desirous of immediately establishing a Mission. In 1822,
Mr. Ephraim Bacon, and his wife, both of whom had
been in Africa in connection with the American Colonization Society, on their return, offered their services
for the commencement of the undertaking. It was
determined to send them out, and to give Mr. Bacon
the appointment of catechist. He employed some months
preparatory to his departure in visiting different parts
of the country for the purpose of exciting an interest in
the Mission, and collecting the necessary funds for its

maintenance. In this he was more successful than had been anticipated ; collecting about eighteen hundred dollars in cash, and a variety of clothing and other useful articles. The way now seemed open for further effort, but an unexpected obstacle arose from the refusal of the Colonization Society, from some motive connected with the internal affairs of their colony at that period, to allow Mr. Bacon's family and the goods procured for the Mission, a passage in their vessels. Another opportunity was then anxiously sought, but in vain ; and at length, all the means which could be used having been adopted without any prospect of success, the Mission was, for the time, with great reluctance on the part of the Executive Committee, abandoned. The money which had been contributed for this object was invested as part of the Foreign Mission fund on account, and was solemnly pledged to the endowment of the African Mission whenever it should be established.

Some years passed away, during which the Executive Committee were not able to obtain the services of a suitable missionary. At length, at a special meeting of the Board of Directors in October, 1827, Mr. Jacob Oson, a colored man who had for several years resided at New Haven, Connecticut, whose character and qualifications for the work were of the most satisfactory kind, and who had been, for some time, a candidate for holy orders in that diocese, was appointed to the service. He was ordained deacon on the 16th of February, 1828, and priest on the following day, by the Rt. Rev. Bishop Brownell. The Board of Directors of the American Colonization Society, offered him a free passage in one of their vessels, and pledges for his support were received, chiefly from individuals of St. Paul's Church, Boston, to the amount of three hundred and sixty dollars per annum. The friends of Africa rejoiced in the hope that the way for the establishment of the Mission was now opened, but they were again disappointed. The summons to prepare for his departure, found Mr. Oson upon a bed of sickness, from which, before the sailing of the vessel, he was carried to the grave.

In 1828, an attempt was made to establish a Mission School at Hartford, for the purpose of training up colored young men to act as teachers and missionaries in Africa. Three or four candidates presented themselves, who were placed under the tuition of an under-graduate of Trinity College, and superintended by the president. With one exception, however, they were found deficient in even the rudiments of an ordinary English education, nor did they answer the expectations formed of their religious character. Although general publicity had been given to the project, no more applications were received ; and the funds of the institution being very limited, the enterprise was necessarily abandoned.

Notwithstanding their repeated disappointments, the Executive Committee of our Missionary Society did not relinquish their benevolent designs towards Africa ; but seeing no reasonable prospect of the immediate accomplishment of their object, they resolved that the articles collected by Mr. Bacon, many of which were likely to be injured while lying useless on their hands, should be transferred to the American Colonization Society, to be disposed of for the benefit of the poor Africans, as origi-

nally designed by the donors. That they still retained
an unskaken conviction of the importance and the prac-
ticability of establishing a Mission in Africa, is abundantly
proved in their repeated and earnest appeals to the
Church in their Annual Reports. In 1833, after refer-
ing to the discouraging circumstances which had hitherto
baffled their efforts, they say : " In the meantime, it is
well known to the Board, that the favorable hand of
God has been continually removing or mitigating the
obstacles which have hindered the establishment of
Christianity on the coast of Africa." They revert to
" the peculiar obligations, under which we, as Americans, lie to the ignorant and miserable race, whose for-
tunes are so closely and so sadly connected with our
own," and recommend " the appointment, as soon as
suitable persons may offer, of two misionaries at the
colony of Liberia and its vicinity."

In the same year, the Committee were informed by
Dr. James Hall, the governor of the colony at Cape
Palmas, that a portion of the most respectable inhabitants of Monrovia, had formed themselves into a religious society, under the title of St. James' Church ; profes-
ing to be governed by the laws of the Protestant Episcopal
Church in the United States of America.   Dr. Hall
placed in the hands of the Committee an appeal for aid
in the erection of a house of worship for said Church,
signed by its Wardens and Vestry. This the Committee
published in the Missionary Record, and in answer to it
received the sum of $201 15. The writer of this appeal
was Mr. James Thompson, Secretary to the Colonial
agent at Cape Palmas. He was a native of Demarara,

about twenty-seven years of age, intelligent, pious, well
educated, ardently attached to the distinctive principles
and features of the Episcopal Church, and, for a considerable period, had been officiating among the colonists
as Lay Reader.   Soon after the meeting of the Board
in 1834, the Secretary of the Society was requested to
open a correspondence with Mr. Thompson, and ascertain from him whether he would be willing to engage
in the service of the Society as an ordained missionary,
provided it was practicable to effect his ordination in
accordance with the canons of the Protestant Episcopal
Church in the United States.   To this inquiry, Mr.
Thompson replied, that he did not consider his qualifications of such a nature as would justify him in assuming
the ministerial office, and would prefer co-operating with
the Society in the capacity of a teacher.   He proposed
a plan for a Mission school which the Committee resolved to adopt.   In June, 1835, they appointed Mr. and
Mrs. Thompson to the office of teachers, and appropriated
a sum for the erection of the necessary buildings.   In
the following Autumn, the managers of the American
Colonization Society, announced to the Secretary of the
Domestic and Foreign Missionary Society, a resolution
of that body, instructing their Colonial agent to grant
to the Society a lot of ground on Factory Island, or elsewhere, within the territory of Liberia.   For this generous
donation, a vote of thanks was promptly transmitted by
the Foreign Committee, who instructed Mr. Thompson to
select such a spot as he should deem most suitable for the
establishment of the proposed Mission school.   Mr.
Thompson was then residing at Cape Palmas, and, after

consultation with Gov. Hall and the Rev. M. Wilson, he decided to locate the Mission in that vicinity. The spot selected was a beautiful mount about three miles distant from the Cape, and situated on the main road leading from the town of Harper to the Cavalla river. Its elevation was about one hundred feet, commanding a fine view of the surrounding country, and affording a distant glimpse of the ocean. The grant included an extent of ten acres.

On the 1st of March, Mr. Thompson commenced his operations in behalf of the Society, and proceeded to clear up the ground, and prepare it for the erection of suitable buildings for the accommodation of a Mission family and school. The work of instruction was commenced immediately, with seven children, five boys and two girls. With the former, Mr. Thompson removed to a small native house on the premises, in order to give his personal attention to the building and other operations, leaving the girls under the care of his wife, at Harper. On Sundays he joined his family, and held religious services, which were frequently attended by the Governor and settlers of the colony.

CHAPTER II.

THUS, after a long series of disappointments, the Church
had, at last, the satisfaction of seeing this much desired
Mission family commenced. Further encouragement was
soon afforded by a letter received from Mr. John Payne,
then a student in the Theological Seminary of Virginia,
offering to engage in the service of the Mission, as soon
as he should be ordained. In August, a similar offer was
received from Rev. Lancelot B. Minor. Both these gentlemen belonged to the Diocese of Virginia, and, being
recommended by their Bishop, were immediately appointed missionaries to Africa. In the same month,
letters were received from the Rev. Thomas S. Savage,
M. D., of Connecticut, expressing an earnest desire to
engage in the same field. His application was also
accepted, and he was desired to be ready to sail in the
autumn, in order that he might be able to make such
arrangements for the reception of the other members of
the Mission, as he might deem necessary for their health
and comfort. For this duty he was especially qualified

by his medical knowledge, which, in view of the peculiar dangers of the African climate, rendered his services particularly valuable. In October, Dr. Savage was ordained to priest's orders by the Rt. Rev. Bishop Brownell, and, on the 1st of November, 1836, he set sail in the brig Niobe, from Baltimore, for Cape Palmas. He arrived at his place of destination on Sunday, December 25th, and, in his first letter to the committee, thus writes :

"I am much pleased with Mr. and Mrs. Thompson. They have a very interesting school of native boys and girls. Every thing connected with the Mission gives evidence of their faithfulness and capability to fill the important post with which they have been intrusted. ********. God has signally blessed us in raising up such servants. In their self-denying labors, he sends over a voice to the Church at home, for the prayer of faith—for persevering effort—for greater self-denial and greater consecration of money, body and soul, to the great work of Africa's redemption. Christians of America ! oh ! will you not hear ? You owe Africa a debt, and one which can never be paid till her long lost sons are restored to her pleading arms. Yes ! Christians of America ! you owe Africa a debt, and one which can never be paid till you have carried the word of God into every family within her borders. ' Freely you have received, freely give.' ******.

"How did I find him (Mr. Thompson) employed ? His school, as has been his custom every Sabbath, was assembled at his house, at the Cape, and a few others, with his own family, were pouring out upon the altar

which he has consecrated to God, the sweet incense of
prayer and thanksgiving. Oh ! never shall I, to my last
breath, forget the emotions which swelled my bosom on
this occasion. I blessed God for having afforded me the
sight, and in the full tide of feeling which delighted my
soul, I once more joyfully vowed to live to His service upon these bleeding, benighted shores."

Under date of January 13th, 1837, he again writes :
"I am highly pleased with our location, and warmly
approve its selection for the commencement of our Missionary operations. Cape Palmas is high and prominent, and, since my arrival, has been visited every hour
of the day with a cool and refreshing breeze. Its pro-
jection into the sea is about one hundred rods, and its
heighth, one hundred feet. It forms, as you are aware,
the turning point from the windward to the leeward
coast. Its relative position, in regard to the interior
and other important points upon the coasts, as well as
other considerations, which will hereafter be mentioned,
lead us to anticipate great facilities in our subsequent
operations, and fully convince me of the propriety of its
selection as our starting point. The bar and landing
are said to be the best in all Western Africa. In this
respect it has certainly the advantage of Bassa Cove,
where landing with small boats is attended with
danger.

" The Cape, itself, is mostly occupied with houses
belonging to the agency and other colonists. Commencing with the main land is a native town, consisting of fifteen hundred inhabitants. The houses or huts
are constructed as follows : Narrow strips of boards,

four or five feet in height, three or four inches wide, and half an inch thick, are placed, perpendicularly, in the ground, arranged in the form of a circle. This constitutes the base; upon this structure is placed the roof, which is made of the leaves of the palm-tree, running up high to a point, very much in the manner of a sugar loaf. This town has its greegree house, i. e. buildings in which are performed their religious ceremonies. These, I am informed, are of the most disgusting character, and are addressed solely to the devil. Their religion is, most emphatically, a religion of devils. On my arrival, I was visited, a number of times, by the king, whose English name is Tom Freeman. Every *gentleman* is thus honored, and were he not apprised of the real motives which prompt to these attentions, he would place these people upon an equality in politeness with some other nations far more advanced in civilization. I have often been surprised with the salutation of a genteel bow, accompanied with a graceful wave of the hand. 'The visits of the king, upon the arrival of a ' gentleman,' as they style every one bringing goods, are made with the expectation of receiving a dash or present. This is in accordance with a long established custom, and so firm is its hold upon their affections, that a compliance becomes a necessary preliminary step to a desirable influence among them, and, consequently, to our usefulness. On returning the king's visit, the first object that attracted my eye was a small stick, about five feet in height, and an inch in diameter, standing at the entrance of his hut. This is his ' greegee pole.' The charm consists in having a few fibres of the inner

2

bark of some tree, dyed black, suspended from the top. Here, night and day, the charm exerts its wondrous power, as it performs a thousand mysterious motions, moved to and fro by the four winds of heaven. I asked the king, through an interpreter, its object. He replied, ' It is my fetish to keep off the witches—the devil-man.' ' What keeps them from me?' said I, ' I have no fetish hung up at my door, no greegee around my person.' A French shrug, with a shake of the head, was the only sign of a reply. I then asked the king if he had ever seen this devil-man, and what he was like? ' He looks black, like countryman,' said he, smiling. ' How do you tell him from your subjects, then,' said I. A hearty laugh was his only answer. After some further remarks, by which I endeavored to make him see the absolute folly of these superstitions, without directly, and perhaps rudely, attacking them, I left him with a heart truly pained at his benighted condition, ******** ******.

" Both these stations (those of the American Board* and of the Methodists) are situated within a few rods of the beach, having the ocean upon the east. Immediately upon the west, is the Maryland Avenue, commencing about this point, and ending at our station. Our location is more to the interior than any of the others, with a distance of two miles between, and three from the Cape. Upon either side of the Avenue are located the emigrants as they arrive.

" We have now about ten acres of land under cul-

---

* This station was subsequently abandoned, the A. B. C. F. M removing their Mission to the Gaboon river.

tivation, planted with the delicious yam, banana, cassada, and plantain, the tangah, sweet potato, and arrow-root, limes, oranges, and palm-trees ; a few American vegetables and fruits, such as tomatoes, egg plant, ocra, cucumbers, Lima beans, musk and water melons, &c., &c.

"The whole of the original grant is now enclosed with an African fence, the best in the colony. The sticks answering to posts, are of the species of a tree very tenacious of life ; (in this respect something like the American salix or willow ;) and, in the course of a few years, will become flourishing trees. As a substitute for rails, sticks of a smaller size are taken and connected by a withe at the end to the posts."

While every thing appeared thus flourishing in the outward aspect of the Mission, encouragement was also offered of a still more gratifying character. Towards the close of his letter Dr. Savage adds :

"An increasing interest is manifested by the children in whatever is told them about God, their Creator and Father in heaven, and Christ their Saviour. On some occasions, some of them have been affected even to tears. This is especially the case with John Thompson and his sister Susan. The former has been with Mr. Thompson about two years, and the latter, sixteen months. On one occasion, when Mr. T. was explaining the nature and design of the Lord's Supper, John wept at the recital of that tale of undeserved love ; and again, while Mrs. T. was reading and explaining some points in the history of Jacob and Joseph, both he and his sister were deeply affected, and shed tears, as many

others have done, over the severe trials of the patriarch
and his favorite son. These are not the exhibitions of
an evanescent feeling, originating merely in the elo-
quence of the speaker, for there is nothing in the manner
of either Mr. or Mrs. T. to produce such an effect ; but
the results of prayerful instruction, now beginning, as
we trust, to receive the promised blessing : a result as
necessarily following such a course of labor as the
golden harvest follows the industry of the husbandman.
I desire to give one interesting circumstance in regard to
Susan, and employ Mrs. Thompson's words. "Whatever art she has been taught, she endeavors to perform
well ; listens attentively to religious instruction, and is
very fond of hearing anything about God and Jesus
Christ. After hearing Mr. Wilson preach to the natives
about the good and evil designs in man's heart, showing
that we have two hearts, one bad, the other good, she
remarked to me, ' I know that very well.' To use her
own words : ' T'other day I do something bad too ; I
scold other girl plenty ; (the word plenty in the Africo-
American dialect, means a great deal ;) my heart be mad
too much. When they wash clothes they make play
plenty—they no wash clothes clean ; then I say some bad
word ; when I done speak 'em, then my heart sorry too
much ; I go garden—I cry plenty—plenty.' At another
time, seeing a native funeral pass, she remarked, ' He
make my heart sorry too much, when country man die.'
On asking her why, she replied, ' Because they no sabby God ;' (know or understand God) ' They no sabby
God book too. I want to live with you, so I can sabby
God proper."

"There is a seed-time and a harvest in the moral, as well as in the natural world, and patience, with a firm trust in the promises and good providence of God, are as requisite in the one, as in the other. Never did I so fully realize the force of this truth as since my foot has pressed a heathen soil, It cannot be too familiar to the minds of Christians at home, but more especially, of the missionary himself. 'Behold,' says the Apostle, 'the husbandman waiteth for the precious fruits of the earth, *and hath long patience* for it, until he receive the early and the latter rain. Be ye also patient ; establish your hearts for the coming of the Lord draweth nigh.' We believe the precious seed of divine truth to be taking effect in the hearts of, at least, the two children above mentioned. If they are permitted to remain with us, we can but feel that they will yet become Christ's by adoption and grace. But alas! there is a possibility of Susan's withdrawal from beneath our instruction and care. It has been a custom, from time immemorial, among this people, and which is almost universally observed, to betroth their daughters in infancy ; in other words, *to sell them.* For a stipulated sum between the father and the other party, the *former* binds himself to deliver over to the *latter* his daughter, whenever he shall make the demand. The age of the proposed husband never becomes a question. It is *the amount to be paid*, which constitutes the pivot upon which the contract turns. Susan, our most interesting and promising scholar in the female department, is a victim to this horrid custom. She is engaged to an old man in the interior, or ' bush,' as the natives term it.

We can redeem her by paying the estimated amount for
which she is sold ; this is about twenty dollars. By
thus redeeming a child both parents and guardians lose
all power and right of control, and she remains for the
future subject solely to our direction and influence. I
will close by mentioning one cruel custom which has
grown out of this horrid practice of betrothing their
children. When the girl is called for by the person who
bought her in infancy, she is obliged to go whether willing
or not. If she refuse, a number of other children are
compelled to whip her into compliance. While at Mr.
Wilson's, a few days since, I was shocked and pained at
the sight of one of these cruel scenes. Six or eight
children were most cruelly lashing the bare back of a
girl, apparently about thirteen years of age, while both
parents, one preceding and the other following, gave direction to the whole affair. There is no alternative between submission or death. Oh ! could one benevolent
female at home witness that sight, but for a moment,
thought I, how soon would she be snatched from the
cruel destiny !"

    The custom here referred to, proved a serious obsta-
cle in the way of establishing female schools. Girls were
liable, at any time, to be withdrawn from instruction, and
forced to swell the retinue of a heathen polygamist. A
step so opposed to the principles in which they had been
educated, could hardly fail to obliterate from their minds
all the influences of the christian religion, and could be
regarded only as a return to heathenism. To redeem
every girl received into the Mission School, so as to acquire
the undisputed right to retain her as long as they pleased,

seemed to the missionaries the only alternative. This
course might seem to countenance the odious custom,
and to some, it appeared wholly objectionable ; yet, if it
were not taken, all hope of benefiting the degraded
females of Africa must be abandoned It was, therefore, finally adopted, and all girls now received into the
Mission, are either secured by the payment of the betrothment money to the parents, or redeemed from a
former purchaser.

At the same time, a written pledge is given by the
missionary for her support and education, promising also,
that as soon as she reach a suitable age, she shall be disposed of in marriage.   In this way wives are secured
for the boys, and many happy couples now rejoice in
their emancipation from the cruel custom of their fathers.

CHAPTER III.

On the 4th of March, the Mission family removed
from the Cape to Mt. Vaughan ; so called in honor of the
Rev. John A. Vaughan, under whose adminstration, as
Secretary of the Board, the enterprise had been commenced. Easter was the day selected upon which to
enter fully upon their Missionary operations.

Dr. Savage now decided upon paying a visit to two
neighboring kings, whose children were members of the
school. The following extract from his journal contains
much useful and interesting information :

"April 14th, 1837. On the morning of the 4th
instant I embarked, in company with Mr. Thompson,
the children who were natives of_that region, and six
Kroomen,* in a canoe, upon Sheppard's Lake, for Grah-

---

* The term "Krooman," is, without doubt, derived from the
original name of the tribe inhabiting the region around Settra
Kroo, which is "Karoo." They were the first to leave their native country and act the part of servants and boatmen along the

way; a town situated upon the coast, at a distance of about eight miles to the leeward of Cape Palmas. This lake is a beautiful sheet of water, extending about eight miles. It is nearly parallel, throughout, with the sea-coast, from which it is separated, in many places, only by a narrow bank of sand thrown up by the surf; thus evidently showing that, originally, it was but a bay, or arm of the sea. Large quantities of fine fish are obtained once or twice during the year, by draining the lake. This is done by a collection of native boys, who, with their hands and sticks, dig a trench in the narrowest part of the bank towards the ocean, when the rush of waters soon breaks an outlet into the sea. A bank is again raised by the returning surf, and the usual quantity of water, soon renewed by the rains and tributary streams. An excursion upon this lake, affords to the admirer of nature, a scene of beauty and surpassing interest. Its banks are mantled with perpetual verdure of the richest hue. From their sloping sides ascend those trees which give to a tropical country its striking and unique appearance. The palm, the pride of tropical

coast. The name was, for some time, confined to them, till, by the enlistment of others, it has become generic. The Krooman's mark consists of a line of dark blue color beneath the cuticle, drawn from between the eyes on the forehead to the tip of the nose, about the eight of an inch in width; and a figure something in the form of a spear head, its point in conjunction with the outer angle of the eye, and extending backward upon the temples. Slaves dare not buy nor steal any one bearing this mark, for so dependent are they upon their agency, that the consideration of their vengeance as the probable consequence, restrains this act of cupidity.

2*

climates, rivals all others in the grandeur of its appearance ; ascending to a height of twenty, forty, sixty, and even a hundred feet, it confines all its foliage to its very summit. I have seen four species in this vicinity. And here, it may not be improper to give a short account of the practical uses of the palm among the natives.

"The palm affords a nut, which, to the Africans, is at once, a great source of food and wealth. When ripe, it is a rich and delicious fruit, possessing a good degree of nutriment. From this nut is obtained the palm oil, which is every year becoming in commerce a more important article of export. The demand is steadily increasing in Europe and America, inasmuch as it is made the basis of the refined and cosmetic soaps. The process by which it is obtained, though rude, is simple, and involves the principles of like operations in all civilized countries. The nuts are gathered at certain seasons, carried to a convenient watering place, then bruised in a mortar, and poured into a canoe of cold water. The pulp is then agitated and squeezed by the hand till all the oil which can be thus expressed, floats upon the surface. It is then skimmed off, and put in earthen pots and jars of native manufacture, for use and market. It is now in its crude state ; and is so used for food and other purposes by the colonists and natives. Its color is a deep yellow, approaching to red. When clarified, it is as colorless as lard, and then forms an oil for the table, not inferior to that of the olive. The price of the oil here, is one dollar, or two bars (of tobacco) for a croo. The nominal value of a bar is fifty cents. The volume of a croo is four gallons. With a slight degree of clarification, palm oil is equal, and many think superior, for light, to any obtained from the whale. It is much cheaper, and we hope ere long, will be offered for sale in that state which is proper for the lamp. Besides the oil, a fluid is obtained from this species, which, as it is drawn from the tree, is sweet and highly pleasant to the taste. This is the native wine of Africa. Within twenty-four hours it undergoes the process of fermentation, and then contains about the same proportion of alcohol as American cider. If carried still farther, it forms a very sharp and pleasant vinegar, inferior, however, to that made from the juice of the apple. The other species of palm, common to this region, are, the palmetto, very much like the cabbage of the South, in the United States,—and the cocoa-nut.

"A no less striking object, on near approach, is the Mangrove,—Rhisophora,—a tree as full of mystery in modern, as in ancient times. One great peculiarity is, the habit of shooting its branches into the water and earth below, forming new trunks and trees, till whole forests thus spring up, within the dark recesses of which, crocodiles and other aquatic animals find a lurking-place. From these mangrove-forests, these hiding-places of water serpents and other reptiles, proceed those nameless things, which seem to have their origin and place, in the theory only, of some medical authors, the tales of travellers, and the Peter Parley's of the day. They are represented as coming forth in millionary numbers, and, with the blight of their wings, spreading far and wide the seeds of disease and death

in the atmosphere of Africa.   These invisible, infinitesi-
mal creatures, or principles, I need not say, I have been
unable to see or detect.   No one, nor all, of my senses,
have yet proved adequate to such a task.   They remain,
therefore, as I found them, in the books and brains of
others.   I can find no other ground for disease, in a
general sense, than what exists in a change of climate,—
its necessary effect upon the system of strangers.   And
as to local causes, they do not differ, so far as I can see,
from those which facts prove to be common in all new
countries.   These, I find sufficient to account, primarily,
for all the disease I have yet seen, peculiar to Africa.
Add to these, the dissipated habits of some, and the
great imprudence of others, and it will be unnecessary
to look much farther for causes of disease.

   "After a delightful sail of about two hours, we arrived
at the town of Grahway, or Grahway Point. Its entrance, like almost all the towns of Western Africa
along the coast, is guarded by a 'greegree house.'
This, generally, consists of two bee-hives, decorated
with feathers, goat horns, rags, &c.   Trees are generally seen, too, with refuse of all kinds thrown around
the roots, and guarded from the contact of profane hands
and feet by a high paling.   These senseless things are
objects of great veneration with the Africans, and are
supposed to exert an influence in warding off, and ap-
peasing the anger, and conciliating the favor of evil spirits.   We found the king of this town absent; and were
received, therefore, by his head trademan.   I asked
what good these things without life could do.   The re
ply was, 'great deal; the people be bad people,—the

devil get among them, so they kill one another,—and
some be sick,—sick head, sick leg, and ebery ting bad,—
bad too much; we send for devil man (doctor) he come,
—he put up greegee,—he cure 'em all,—no sick now,—
all ting go on fine,—be good people,—and dat de good
they do.' Soon, this wonderful man appeared, and a formal introduction took place between the African and the
American Doctor. The African insignia of his office
are, a long, bushy beard, and a monkey skin thrust under his left arm. These poor deluded people had sent
nearly a hundred miles up the coast, for the services of
this celebrated agent of the Evil One."

"The manner of inducting a candidate into this important office is as follows. The individual is first
seized with a violent shaking or ague all over. In this
condition he continues, at intervals, for several months.
In the meantime he becomes solitary and abstracted,
communing with himself in an unintelligible jargon.
His friends, after some difficulty, extract from him the
secret cause of his malady. He declares that the Devil
has called him to be a doctor, and has threatened heavy
calamities to himself and his people should he refuse the
office. He is then recommended to study the art, and
various ceremonies are performed by way of introducing
him to his preparatory course. Among others, his head
is shaved, and his hair deposited with the man whom
he first acquaints with his call. He then attaches himself to one or more regular fetish men, and spends several months, perhaps a year or two, in studying the
various remedies for disease, manner of preparing greegrees, &c. During his novitiate, he is permitted to wear

no clothing except such as is made from monkey skins or grass, nor is he allowed to wash, except in the rain. At the expiration of this period, he returns to his friends, accompanied by his preceptor. A large meeting of Devil-men is called, and numerous ceremonies are again thought necessary before he can be inducted into office. The grand test is to be made of his proficiency in the sublimest mysteries of the craft. The head of a dog is cut off and secreted in a jungle ; and he is commanded to find it. The instructor and his pupil place themselves in the centre of a circle, formed by a large number of spectators. The Devil is invoked, and all the resources of the magic art are employed. On a sudden, the candidate shakes violently, leaps up, and is driven, by a supernatural impulse, to the spot where the dog's head was concealed. He returns in triumph with the trophy, and becomes licensed to trade in all the ' lying wonders' of his profession. Women, as well as men, are admitted to this office."

From Grahway Dr. Savage and his party continued their journey to the next considerable town, Half Cavalla, distant about six miles. Leaving the beach here, they struck what is called a bush path, designing to take canoes at a given point upon the Cavalla River, and descend to King Baphros', whose town, Grand Cavalla, is at its mouth. " By this course," he continues in his journal, " we passed through a succession of rich bottomed lands and beautiful meadows, more fertile, if possible, than any yet seen. Here we saw whole orchards of the finest plantains, pawpaws, bananas, &c. Many of the former were, at least, thirty feet high.

Lime trees, with their rich foliage and golden fruit, most beautifully diversified the scene. As we approached the towns, groups of natives would surround us, with bowls filled with the delicious fruits of the region, and urging them upon our acceptance."

From such facts, one is disposed to look upon the Africans as the most hospitable people in the world. When, however, you are about to leave them, they fail not to beg for more than an equivalent for their hospitalities. The Cavalla is a beautiful river, skirted by the same trees which I have seen along the banks of other rivers on other parts of the coast ; such as the mangrove, the teak, dragon's blood and others, with a variety of shrubs peculiar to a tropical region, presenting a scene of vegetation of the richest possible verdure. It varies from three fourths, to a mile, in width, is fresh to its very mouth, and flows with great rapidity ; so much so, that its immense volume of water, meeting the swell of the ocean, causes a fearful surf, which breaks, with the roar of thunder, upon the beaten shore. This river is of considerable importance to us in our future operations upon the interior. It penetrates to an unknown extent.

Nations, for a long distance up, are known to inhabit its banks, who have no hope and are without God in the world ; thousands and tens of thousands sunk in the deepest moral degradation ; *cannibals*—human beings who devour the flesh, and drink the blood of their fellow men, live within one hundred miles of the mouth of the Cavalla River ; within two hundred miles of the Christian settlement, the Missionary Station at Cape Palmas.

This river will convey, upon its swelling bosom, to their very doors, the law of God. * * * * * Oh! where are the devoted, self denying sons of God,—where are the disciples of the meek and lowly Jesus, whom he commanded to "Go into all the world and preach the Gospel to every creature?" Are they slumbering over the miseries, the fearful condition of these Africans? Are they *slumbering* in *the fold of Christ*, the arms of Jesus, when the soul-agonizing cry of millions daily ascends towards heaven for the bread of life? No, no! this cannot be. *It is not.* The arms of Jesus embrace no soul who feels not as he felt, who weeps not as he wept, over the ruined, undying souls of men. He came to save such as these—for these, he came to die. And it is such as these, whom his followers must go to save—for these, they must be willing even to *die.* "If any man have not the spirit of Christ he is none of his."

As one object of Dr. Savage in visiting the kings, was to prove to them his desire to do them and their children good, he held a short exhibition in their presence, consisting of exercises in reading, reciting, enumerating, &c. The effect upon the Baphro is thus described: "During the exercises of the boys, deep emotion was visible in every feature and action. He changed his seat three times, and his posture, many more. One moment he would stand erect, wrapt in thought, without the movement of a muscle; then he would throw himself upon his couch, and, extended at full length, give vent to his emotions through large volumes of smoke, as they rolled from his pipe. When our short exercises were over, Baphro rose, and slowly folding his arms, said, in a deep, solemn tone, ' white man know ebery ting. Black man know noting. All he eber know come from white man. My old fader live here, and die a fool. I live here, and I die a fool, but dat boy (pointing to his son,) he know someting. Ah! white man pass black man. White man be good—he come to do black man good. Yes! white man live in my heart, and all he do live, in my heart too, (putting his hand on his breast in an emphatic manner,) and I be white man's friend.' "

The expression, " live in my heart," implies the warmest approbation. Leaving Grand Cavalla, Dr. Savage extended his journey eight or nine miles further along the coast, to Rockbookah. Here he was kindly received, and as the exercises of the scholars were witnessed, by a larger number, the expressions of pleasure and surprise were proportionally louder.

CHAPTER IV.

DR. SAVAGE returned to Mt. Vaughan, quite encouraged by the friendly feeling which had been evinced by the people, and their repeated requests for the establishment of schools. In subsequent excursions in other directions, he found the desire for instruction universally prevalent. It is true that this desire arose from no sense of their moral and religious degradation, for, having no idea of sin *as an offence against God*, they could have no consciousness of the need of the Gospel. Although acknowledging a Supreme Being, called Gnisuah, the Africans have no conception of his character and attributes. He is regarded by them as the Creator, but not as the Governor of the universe. This they seem to regard as given up to the dominion of the prince of darkness, who is the sole object of their worship. The whole aim of their religious ceremonies seems to be to turn away the wrath of this dreaded being ; and their lives are passed in continual fear of his malign influences. The existence of subordinate evil spirits is also acknow-

ledged, and these share their superstitious reverence
and fear. But while indifferent to the glad tidings of
the heralds of salvation, they cannot but see and ac-
knowledge the superiority of the Europeans; and desire,
as they express it in their own vague manner, to "sabby
book," that they may be "fine like white man." "They
wish," says Dr. Savage, "to know the white man's
God, because they think by so doing they shall become
the white man's equal : and this is encouragement to
missionary effort. This is a door—a door opened—
through which the light of the Gospel may be brought
to strike upon their benighted minds."

The journey, of which some account is given above,
was made in April, 1837. The following month, Dr.
Savage pursued his inquiries to Deneh, a town situated
on the Cavalla river, about forty miles from its mouth,
and the same distance from Cape Palmas. A few extracts from his journal, on this occasion, will serve to
throw additional light upon the manners and customs
of the people.

"May 17th, 1837,—Embarked, this morning, about
half past ten o'clock, upon Sheppard's Lake, for 'Grahway Point,' accompanied by Mr. T. and the usual com-
plement of Kroomen. Cool and pleasant—the ther-
mometer standing at 78 degrees in the shade—arrived
at Grahway, and found the inhabitants in great commo-
tion from the following cause : A thunder storm had
occurred two nights before, during which a house was
burnt. Such an event, seen through the medium of superstition, could be the result of nothing short of witchcraft. Hence, according to the usual custom, a consul-

tation was held with the 'Devil,' or 'Greegee man,' and an accusation brought against one of their number. The charge was that of 'calling down lightning from heaven, and maliciously consuming the house of an unoffending citizen!' He confessed his guilt, and, in doing so, implicated two others as his abettors. The result was, as usual, the administration of the 'red water.' It is supposed to be very poisonous. It cannot be so, however, for the great quantity required to destroy life, proves that it is but moderately deleterious. The bulk of fluid itself, would be sufficient, in many cases, to produce death. It is, however, the cause of death to thousands in this heathen land.

"The man who confessed, had taken his portion before our arrival, and having escaped its fatal effects was now going at large through the town. I asked the principal actor in this scene, if he really believed that man capable of doing what had been charged against him. His reply was, "spose him no do him, tink him say yes, when he know it be sassy wood palaver? Ugh! I no tink so." They have another custom which, I hope, proved the means of arresting all farther proceedings in this diabolical affair. It is this. If a stranger of distinction arrive at the time, the criminal is entitled to an escape. Being viewed in this light by them, I have reason to believe that I was the means of saving one of the two implicated, from a cruel death.

"The 'red water' here referred to, is a poisonous decoction made from the bark of a tree, (a species of laurel,) and administered as a test of guilt or innocence, in accusations of crime. In a concentrated form, it is a powerful narcotic, and in larger quantities, an emetic. The idea involved in the administration is, that a spirit accompanies the draught, and searches the heart of the suspected individual for his guilt. If he be innocent, the spirit returns with the fluid in the act of ejection, but if guilty, it remains to do more surely the work of destruction."

Dr. Savage passed the first night of his journey at Nallicott, a town about three miles from the mouth of the Cavalla ; and gives the following account of an incident which occurred the next morning. " We left Nallicott in two canoes, our Kroomen keeping time, with their paddles, to one of their rude, but not unpleasant songs. We had not proceeded far, when the cry of ' Snake in the tree !' ' Snake in the tree !' was heard, and a serpent was discovered on a branch directly over our heads. Every arm was now exerted to the utmost, and our frail bark literally darted from beneath our dangerous foe. The feeling excited by this occurrence had no sooner subsided, than another cry was heard,—' Snake crosses the river !' and another was seen wending his way to the opposite side. These reptiles are objects of great dread to the Africans. Their bite is said to be fatal. Their habit is to ascend an overhanging tree and suddenly dart into the passing canoe. When this happens the natives invariably abandon it.

" A highly attractive object to my New England eye, was maize, so frequently seen upon the banks of this river ; and another, no less reviving my southern associations, was rice ; both of which are produced here in perfection.

" We arrived at Hedia at 12 o'clock. It is called Grand Devil Town, from the fact that Grand Devil Place is within its limits, and that here, resides the priest who performs the ceremonies attending all visits of inquiry. This town may be called the Delphi of Western Africa ; the Grand Devil Place, its oracle, standing in very much the same relation to the inhabitants, as Delphi, in ancient Greece, to that country. I have often made inquiries respecting the degree of influence which this imposture has upon the minds of the natives, and have discovered that, among the older ones, it is regarded with feelings of mystery and reverence; but its hold upon the younger, is more feeble. It subserves the same purposes as the oracle of olden time ; success or failure in matters of high moment are divined, and the accomplishment of a given desire, either public or private, secured."

We interrupt the course of the Dr's. Journal here, to introduce some further account of the same spot afterwards given by another missionary.*

"The shrine of the oracle, as I have been informed by those who visited it, is a large perpendicular rock, with a cavity in the centre, from which leads a hole or fissure to the top. The priest secretes himself within this cavity, and the fissure serves as the channel of communication. When all things are prepared, a colloquy something like the following ensues :

" *Priest.* Well, you no come here for war greegee— did you ?

" *Answer.* No !

* Rev. Mr. Henning.

"*P.* You no come for sick greegee?

"*A.* No!

"*P.* You no come for woman palaver?

"*A.* No!

"*P.* You no come for trade greegee?

"*A.* No!

"*P.* Well; what did you come for?

"*A* I come for fish greegee!

"*P.* Well; didn't I tell you so first time? What for you no say so? Answer me right.

"The simple dupe retires, awe-struck by the reflection, that his most secret thoughts have been read by the great magician."

"Instances are known," continues Dr. S., "where persons have come, for hundreds of miles, in different directions, for consultation; and certain European traders, who have permanent factories upon the coast, we are informed, have resorted to its impositions to facilitate the accomplishment of their purposes. It is a spot well selected for the object in view, difficult of access, dark and gloomy—circumstances well calculated to inspire the superstitious mind with fear and reverence.

"Leaving Hedia, we were cheered by the fact, that our next stopping place would be Deneh. Here, for the first time, I saw the African monkey. The natives set a high value upon this animal as an article of food. Monkey soup is, to them, what turtle soup is to us. On their 'bill of fare,' and esteemed as delicacies, will be found many things from which the civilized mind shrinks with disgust; such as reptiles, the different kind of vermin, &c. The usual method of taking the monkey is as fol-

lows : When one or more is seen, they are immediately
surrounded by the hunters. Springing from tree to
tree, they chatter, for a time, defiance to their pursuers.
In an unwary moment, they congregate upon another,
more lofty or isolated, near the river bank. The natives
now arrange themselves so as to prevent their escape.
The tree is felled, and the monkeys plunge into the
water. The natives follow, and, being more expert at
swimming, they soon disable their prey with clubs, and
return in triumph to their homes.

" Within two or three miles of Deneh the scenery
begins to change its character. The banks of the river
become more elevated, till, near the town, they are
strikingly so. It was about six o'clock when we found
ourselves drawing near, and seven before we arrived.
The sun had set behind the highlands without a cloud
intercepting its rays ; a rich mellow light overspread the
surface of nature, and softened its wildness to an aspect
of sweet serenity. Even the heathen felt its soft influence. The song of the boatmen had ceased, and
hardly a sound was heard save the rippling of the waters, as our frail bark moved gently onwards. The
news of our coming had preceded us, and watchmen
were on the look out for our approach. Soon the cry
was heard—' Kubi di ! Kubi di ! White man comes !
White man comes !' A small bay opened, and the landing place was discovered, crowded with natives to re
ceive us. I was conducted, fatigued and unwell, to the
house of the king, which was large and comfortable.
Being a white man and a stranger, I was, as usual, an
object of curiosity, and, consequently, annoyed by a

crowd of visitors; I say annoyed, because I was under the mysterious influence of an intermittent. Such circumstances, however, can be made profitable, for they often try, to the utmost, one's patience. At my request that the king would disperse his people, the house was soon cleared, and I was left, for the night, to reflection and repose.

" 19th. Obtained but little rest through the night —quite ill this morning; as the day advanced my health improved. Had an interview with the king, and found him very desirous that schools should be established for his people. He seems mild, pleasant and hospitable, and appears to have the good of his people at heart. Having accomplished my object, as I thought, I designed to leave in the afternoon, in time to reach one of King Tom's towns on the river, and there spend the night. But no sooner was this discovered by my host, than he came into the hut with his head man, and began, in a fervid and eloquent manner, to show me its impropriety. His argument was as follows: 'You be new man— no live in my country long time, him no sabby you proper now—(i. e. is not congenial to your constitution,) you come long way look me—make you sick—spose you go down the river, be bad palaver—make you more sick —you die; then me no look on you more—no! you be sick plenty—you live here to-day, me do you good fash —no man look you—you get sleep—then you be well. My heart no speak all yet; plenty ting live there—that time you be better, then I bring my head men—we speak all palaver about school. Then you sleep next day—plenty men carry you softly through the bush—
3

plenty tree live there—no let sun look you, and you go
home fine.' Such were the sentiments and feelings of
this heathen man, as made known to me through an interpreter. I had no cause to doubt his sincerity."

Dr. Savage accepted the king's invitation to remain
another day, and then commenced his homeward journey.
On his route he visited two or three other towns, where,
however, he was less hospitably received. With a glance
at one or two heathen customs, not yet mentioned, we
conclude our extracts from his journal on this occasion.

"While in Deneh, a woman had fallen under the
suspicion of her husband; twice was she rescued, by us,
from the dreadful punishment inflicted in such cases, viz :
thrusting her hands into a cauldron of boiling oil! If
the wretched victim escape without denuded flesh,
(more often bones in reality,) she is pronounced innocent; but if not, guilty! In the latter case, the administration, to death, of the horrible red water, or sassa
wood, is sure to follow."

"In Barracah, I saw an enclosure about four feet in
height, and as many in diameter, made of sticks, and
filled with beach sand brought upon the heads of the natives, from a point thirty miles distant. I approached,
and, putting my hand into the sand, asked what it was
for. An exclamation of horror burst from the surrounding crowd, and all seemed to look as if they expected me
' to swell or fall down suddenly ;' but after they had
looked a great while and saw no harm come to me, they
changed their minds, and concluded that ' black man's
fetish no fit white man.' ' Fetish no be for white
man,' say they, whenever the folly of their superstition

is thus fully demonstrated,—' Witch can't touch him.'
It seems that this was the public fetish of the Barracah
people, and had been placed in the centre of the town
that it might equally exert its influence over the whole !"

CHAPTER V.

Arrival of Mr. and Mrs. Payne and Mr. Minor—Failure of Dr. Savage's health—Cause—Different dialects of natives—Dr. S. returns to U. S.—Attempt to open a Station at Garraway—Death of Mr. Thompson—Manner of preparing farms.

On the 4th July, 1837, the heart of the lone pioneer was cheered by the arrival of his associates, Mr. Minor and Mr. and Mrs. Payne. Through the blessing of God on his skilful treatment, they all passed through the acclimating fever in safety ; but the accumulation of care and anxiety proved too much for his already enfeebled strength, and, in December following, he was compelled to seek a temporary respite from his labors. The arrival of a vessel bound to Monrovia, afforded him the desired opportunity, and he embarked Dec. 28th, leaving his associates able to assume the charge of the Mission.

In reference to this, he writes : " I do wish the true cause of my illness to be well understood. Till my associates arrived, and for more than a month after, my health was good. They came in the midst of the rainy season. The morning of their arrival saw me walking into the Cape, in health, to meet them. In their eyes, I had not changed. My complexion and general appearance indicated, to them, as good health as I had enjoyed in America. They found me alone, pressed by numerous duties, and themselves upon my hands, the objects of deep anxiety. Such a state of things necessarily continued for a time, and our quinine gone, repeated attacks of the ague and fever brought me low. Hepatic derangements were the sure consequence, bringing, in their train, great suffering and danger of life. It is my firm belief that, under different circumstances, my health would still have been good. I do not believe this climate to be necessarily fatal to the white man's constitution or health. That it involves much, and, often, great suffering, with a thousand circumstances of severe trial, we all cheerfully admit ; and even that life, for years to come, will be shortened by it. Yet it is at the same time no less true, that, with a moderate share of prudence, we can live here and enjoy good health, (though it cannot be permanently as good as we might expect, in our native climate,) and above all, labor for years to save, from eternal death, hundreds and thousands and millions of our fellow beings. *If Christians ask more, they must go to other fields."* * * * * * *

" The interior, in every direction from us, is occupied by populous towns, containing from 1000 to 1500 souls. Indeed, we may extend a line from Cape Palmas, fifty miles into the interior, and, within the arc it would describe from the windward to the leeward coast, we should find, it is estimated, not less than 60 or 70,000 persons, and all willing, to say the least, to receive a teacher. Scattered over this tract of country, we should find many different tribes, with different dialects, yet not so different as to prevent an intelligent Grebo (the tribe at Cape Palmas) from understanding or *being understood* in any other tribe. That all spring originally from the same stock, is evident from the fact that there are many words common to all these dialects, and many more, derived from the same roots. Their numerals exhibit but a shade of difference. The inference then is, that it is highly important to reduce these dialects to a common written language."*

When Dr. Savage embarked from Monrovia, it was with the design of visiting America ; but having learned, on his arrival at that place, that a vessel had passed for Cape Palmas, which he had reason to suppose brought him communications from the Committee, he determined to return to the Cape, and await another opportunity. By this arrangement, his departure for America was delayed until the 30th of April, 1838. He arrived safely in his native land in June following. During his absence, his fellow laborers were actively engaged in the duties of the Mission. A Sabbath school was opened among the natives at the Cape, and the Gospel was regularly preached in the neighboring towns. Some excursions were also made into the interior, in which preliminary steps were taken towards the establishment of inland Stations, but the jealousies existing between the different native tribes, prevented the execution of the plan. The coast people are, generally, hostile to the interior tribes, and unwilling that they should hold any direct intercourse with foreigners. The greatest insult

* Since the above was written, the Grebo language has been reduced to writing, and large portions of the New Testament have been translated.

which can be offered to a coast native is to call him a
" bushman." The articles purchased, by the former,
from the white man, are sold to the latter, at an exorbitant advance, and, as education would enable him to detect the imposition, it is, of course, opposed by his dis-
honest neighbor. It is only by the dissemination of
Christian principles among the natives of the coast, that
this opposition can be overcome.

Another serious drawback upon the operations of
the Mission, was experienced, in this year, from the difficulties which arose between the natives and the American colonists. In the view of the natives, the missionaries were identified with the colonists, and the resentment felt towards the one, under real or imaginary
wrongs, was mutually extended to the other. These
views led to an attempt to establish one or more stations without the boundaries of the colony. In August,
Mr. Minor visited the town of Garraway, on the windward coast, about thirty miles from Cape Palmas, where
his proposal to open a school was favorably received.
When, however, he renewed his visit in September, for
the purpose of completing the arrangement, unexpected
obstacles presented themselves. The Bushmen were
present, and who, for some unexplained reason seemed to
exercise controlling influence, opposed the settlement of
a missionary ; saying that learning was of no use, since it
did not enable a man to get money, and that if Mr.
Minor came, other Americans would come and form a
colony, and that, when a vessel arrived, he would send
" a book " on board and stop the trade in rum, as Dr.
Hall had done at Cape Palmas. Mr. Minor was, therefore, compelled to abandon his design.

The school at Mt. Vaughan continued in a flourishing condition; the male department containing twenty-
five scholars, and the female twelve; all but five, being
the children of natives.   There had been an accession to
the Mission during the year.   Mr. E. S. Byron, a communicant from Grace Church, Boston, was sent out, by
the committee, as an assistant teacher, and Mr. M. Appleby, a young man from Baltimore, was also employed
in the same capicity.   In a letter, dated December,
1838, Mr. Payne notices the death of Mr. James M.
Thompson.   Although, at one time, suspended from the
employment of the Mission, on account of charges affecting his character as a religious teacher, Mr. Thompson gave, in his last illness, gratifying evidence of preparation for the great change.   On the morning before
his death, he expressed, in the last words that he spoke,
his unshaken faith in the promises of God, and a firm
hope of his acceptance through Christ.   Mrs. Thompson's valuable services were secured for the Mission, and
she proved a very efficient teacher in the female department of the school.

In describing one of the journeys made, at this time,
into the interior, Mr. Payne says: "Our road led us
through the section of country which one or two families are preparing for the reception of rice, the present
year.   I had, therefore, a good opportunity of observing
the manner of preparation, and also, of forming some estimate of the industry of the people. The land is cleared
in the following manner.   With a piece of flat iron,
called a bill-hook, they cut out all the grass and under-
growth.   The larger trees are then felled, either by the

small axes of the natives, or by fire. The whole is then suffered to remain until perfectly dry, when fire is communicated, presenting scenes of the most sublime and awful character." The labor of *planting* the farms is principally performed by women. It is a slow and tedious process. Instead of sowing the rice broadcast, they make small holes in the ground with a pointed iron, and deposite a few grains in each, drawing the earth over them with the foot. This is done in April, immediately before the rainy season, which commences in May, and the harvest is reaped in August.

3*

CHAPTER VI.

Sailing of new missionaries—Illness and death of Mrs. Savage—Lines by Mrs. Sigourney.

In December, 1839, the ship Emperor sailed from New-York, taking out the Rev. Dr. Savage and Mr. George A. Perkins, with their wives. Mrs. Savage was the daughter of Mr. John Metcalf, of Fredericksburg, Va., and long an active member of St. George's Church, in that city. Mr. and Mrs. Perkins were communicants of St. Peter's Church, Salem. The friends of the Mission, cheered by this large accession to its numbers, looked forward with sanguine hope, to its increased prosperity and usefulness. But alas! in the mysterious providence of God, they were destined to a severe trial of faith. The very first arrival from the coast, after this little band had landed on its shores, brought the intelligence of Mrs. Savage's death. We extract the following account of this sad event from the Southern Churchman, in which it was published at the time.

"Information of the death of Mrs. Savage, the wife of the Rev. Thomas S. Savage, M. D., one of our missionaries to Cape Palmas, has just been received, and we join, suddenly and sadly, in the general expression of

grief which it has called forth. A long acquaintance
with her bereaved husband, both in college and since,
awakens in us more than common sympathy for him.
May the sanctifying grace of God, of which we are sure
he possesses a more than common share, make this severe
affliction productive of much good here, both to him and
his mission, and an eternal weight of glory hereafter.
Let no Judas among the disciples of Christ ask the question—' For what purpose is this waste?' We doubt not
that this event, caused by an unreserved consecration
on the part of our departed sister, is more precious
and fragrant in the estimation of that Saviour whom she
loved, than that alabaster box of ointment with which
Mary once anointed his feet. ' Blessed are the dead who
die in the Lord.' Here is the consolation for all—her
husband, her parents, and the mission to which she had
devoted herself. She is happy; and if so, who will hesitate to tread in her footsteps? Men of worldly heroism
do not usually retreat from the battle, merely because
they behold a few of their companions falling in the front
ranks. This result is expected, as a matter of course, in
every engagement, and should serve to stimulate those
who are behind, to occupy their places. The death of
every missionary to Africa is like good seed sown upon
good ground. It will spring up and bear much fruit.
Let us, therefore, rejoice that our sister was counted
worthy to suffer for the cause of Christ."

We subjoin the following letters in relation to this
afflictive, but wise dispensation of divine Providence, one
of which is from Mrs. Payne, to a friend in New-York,
dated Cape Palmas, April 21st, 1839.

"I have now a sad and all-engrossing subject to write upon. God, in his wisdom, has seen fit to visit us with a severe affliction. Hitherto, we have written of his goodness in preserving our lives, and I doubt not, though hidden from us, it is equally manifested in the present dark and trying dispensation. Our dear sister, Mrs. Savage, was taken from us on Tuesday last, April 16th, after a severe illness of more than seven weeks. Her sufferings, from the commencement to the end of her illness, were continued and intense; more so than I ever witnessed. Severe, however, as they were, they never elicited a murmur from this lovely Christian. 'I feel that it is all for my good,—not one pain too much,'— was a sentiment frequently expressed. I was permitted the mournful gratification of constantly attending on her sick bed, being kept from her by my own sickness only two days. From the first, she had the impression that her illness would be fatal, and never expressed a wish to recover. An earnest desire to depart and be with Christ was her predominant feeling. About two weeks before her death, she observed: 'I have given up all my friends,—all earthly ties,—my dear husband was·the last I could give up, but I have been enabled to do that now, and know that God will comfort and support him.' Throughout her illness, her mind was in a most tranquil and happy frame. She often said, when I first entered her room in the morning: 'Oh, Anna, I have had such a delightful season,—such sweet views of God and heaven.' The love of the Saviour was a theme upon which she delighted to dwell, and even when too feeble to talk much herself, she took pleasure in hearing others speak of it. 'Go on, dear,' she would say to me, 'I love to hear you talk of the goodness of God.' The last week or two, she was extremely feeble, not able to raise herself in bed, and had several fainting fits. The calm and peaceful state of her mind might be inferred from a little circumstance which occurred the night before her death. The nurse was awakened by some one singing. She arose, and found, to her suprise, that it was Mrs. Savage. She sang, in her sleep, two or three verses of a favorite hymn; the two last lines, the nurse told me, sounded more sweetly than anything she had ever heard. They were:

> ' We're marching through Emmanuel's land,
> To fairer worlds on high.'

May we not imagine that she was then enjoying a fore-taste of the happiness she was soon to realize? When I went in, in the morning, she welcomed me with a sweet smile, and said she felt 'a great deal better,'—an ex-pression she had never before used. I was not, for a moment, deceived; a change had evidently taken place, and I felt my heart sink at the conviction, which I had hitherto striven against, that we must lose her. Through-out the day, her mind was wandering, which it had never been before; still there was nothing distressing about it; all her imaginings were of a pleasurable na-ture, and she knew every one about her. She sunk gradually during the day, and, at half-past eleven at night, fell asleep in Jesus. I was forcibly reminded of the hymn—

> ' Jesus can make a dying bed
> Feel soft as downy pillows are,

> While on his breast I lean my head,
> And breathe my life out sweetly there.'

"Not one struggle,—not one long breath,—but quietly and sweetly as an infant falling to sleep, did she depart. Though holding her hand in mine, I was, for some time, unconscious that she had left us. Almost her last words were, in answer to a question, how the Saviour now appeared to her? 'Chiefest among ten thousand, and altogether lovely.' The funeral took place the next afternoon."

Extract from a Sermon on the death of Mrs. Savage, by the Rev. E. C. McGuire.

"We have dwelt thus far upon the animating topics of the text, as involving a suitable introduction to our intended remarks in reference to one, who, having from infancy, gone in and out among you, and, for some years, been numbered in this congregation with the followers of the Saviour, has recently yielded up her life on a far distant shore, in the honored cause of her ascended Lord and Master. But a brief season has elapsed since we saw her bearing a part in the devotional services of the sanctuary, and in those becoming duties and labors of love which happily engaged so much of the zeal and energy of her pious youth. Called in the midst of these, as she thought, to a more arduous and important field of Christian effort, she did not refuse the path of duty, nor shrink from the open prospect of inevitable hardship and probable mortality. To sever the cherished ties of domestic and social love,—to tear herself away from the friends and home of her youth,—and exchange them for a foreign, barbarous land,—demanded no ordinary exercise of moral purpose, of Christian heroism. But the infirmites of nature yielding to the energies of grace, the resolution was formed for the toils and sacrifices of the missionary cause. With a worthy companion who had devoted himself to the same work of Christ, in an unfriendly clime, she bade adieu to family and friends in November, of the last year, and in the following December left her native shores for the scene of her future abode. Subjected, by a rough and tedious passage, to much bodily suffering, she reached Monrovia on the 19th of January last. From thence, she was enabled to express her filial feelings in a postscript added to a letter written home by her husband. ' I only add a line to say I am better to day than I have been since we left our native shores, and am looking forward, with eager anticipations, to our arrival at home My love, just warm from the heart, to you and my dear mother. May God restore her to health, and spare her useful life for many, many years. Continue ever to pray for us, my dear father. May God preserve our lives and permit us to meet again on earth, and at last unite us around His throne in heaven, is the daily prayer of your devoted daughter.'

"Remaining a few days at Monrovia, the vessel arrived at Cape Palmas on the 29th. With her accustomed diligence, our sister entered upon the duties which awaited her. But scarcely had her domestic arrangements been completed, before the mysterious summons of the grave reached her in a violent attack of acclimating fever. During two tedious months did she meekly endure her painful malady,* cheered by occasional symptoms of convalesence, but mainly oppressed with sufferings so great as to intimate, distinctly, their fatal termination, to herself and others. Whatever could be done by medical skill in the person of a devoted husband, and the untiring assiduities of sympathising female affection, was done to mitigate her trial and avert the melancholy issue, dreaded by them all. But everything was unavailing. About the middle of April the foreboded hour arrived when, nature exhausted by suffering, she sunk into the arms of death, expiring without a sigh or a struggle. The day following, her remains were conveyed to the grave, in a corner of the Mission lot at Mt. Vaughan, where they repose beneath the spreading branches of a few ever verdant palm-trees, within sound of the hoarse Atlantic, filling the ear of night, as it beats upon that fervid shore, with loud and ceaseless murmurs.

" It will, no doubt, gratify many of you, my friends, to learn the spirit and frame of mind in which our departed sister passed through the furnace of affliction, to her reward in heaven. We have abundant reason to bless God for the grace vouchsafed her, in the midst of severe and unwonted trials. That her confidence in Him was not misplaced, we have cheering proofs, manifested from the commencement to the close of her protracted troubles. A favorite devotional book, given her by a friend, contains these grateful indications in sundry passages, carefully marked with a pencil, as expressing sentiments especially selected and adopted by her, as her own.

* Mrs. Savage's sufferings and death cannot be attributed *solely* to the fever.

Among these, we find the following, in which, though dead, she now speaks in words of admonition to those who yet survive.

" ' What proportion, really, is there between the troubles of a moment, and an eternity of glory ? What proportion, between a few drops of gall, and this immense weight of glory ? Let us regard this necessity of suffering as a pleasure and welcome condition. Let us enter, with joy, upon this career in which we follow Jesus; in which so many of all ages, sexes and conditions, have preceded us. They have reached the desired haven. Let us press on, and we shall arrive there too.'

" Again; ' If we suffer with Jesus, we shall also reign with him ; and, to make us sure of it, he calls our sufferings his afflictions. He bore your sins upon the cross ; would you shrink from the rest of his afflictions ?'

" Again : ' In our tribulations we should consult the oracle of our Father, and seeking from him comfort and guidance, we should shed our tears into his bosom, and pour out, in his presence, the bitterness of our souls.'

" With a more cheerful spirit, perhaps, was the following meditation marked : ' Why do you fear to bear the cross which lays open to you the path to heaven ? There is no salvation for the soul, no hope of eternal life, if it be not in the cross. Take up then, thy cross ; follow Jesus and thou shalt attain unto everlasting life. He has gone before thee, bearing his cross, and died upon it that thou mightest bear thy cross, and wish to die upon it. Go where thou wilt, thou canst not find a path more lofty or more sure than the path of the cross.'

"With yet more of triumph, it would seem, she embraced the following thoughts : ' Thou art then, even in this present life, oh ! Christ, my wisdom, my portion, my light, my redemption, my justification, my sanctification, my support and my life, my strength and my defence. But in another life, thou wilt be my perfection, my felicity, my reward.'

" In a congenial frame, and with seemingly prophetic view, does she take up the animated strain—' In this world, how is man defiled with sins, agitated with passions, disquieted with fears, tortured with cares, embarrassed with refinements, deluded with vanities, encompassed with errors, worn out with labors, vexed with temptations, enervated with pleasures and tormented with want. Oh! when will these various evils be no more ? When shall I be delivered from the slavery of sin ? When, O Lord ! shall my thoughts and desires centre and be fixed on thee alone ? Oh ! when will peace return and be established ; peace from the troubles of the world and the disorders of sinful passions—universal peace, incapable of interruption ; that peace which passeth all understanding ? When, oh most merciful Jesus, when shall I stand in pure abstraction from all inferior good, to gaze upon thee, and contemplate the wonders of redeeming love ? Oh ! when shall I dwell with thee in thy kingdom, which thou hast prepared for thy beloved, before the foundation of the world ?'

" In the same devout spirit, with ardent breathings after God, did our deceased sister pass through the severity of her last sickness. With moments of despond-

ency, she yet was permitted to rejoice in days of assurance, of sweet peace and comfort in the Holy Ghost.
Of this period of her decease, her husband writes : 'At
one time, during her first attack, when she thought she
could recover, with tears and groans she said, ' my Sa-
vior hides his face from me.' Before, she had never
spoken, but of his consoling presence. This, however,
was also momentary. I took the Bible, and read a few
verses from the New Testament and the 27th Psalm.
The cloud was cleared up before the eye of faith, and her
swelling soul rejoiced again in Christ. I knew of no
similar doubts after this. She was particularly fond of
the 27th Psalm, and often requested me to read it, saying : 'The Lord is, indeed, my light and my salvation.'
She delighted also in the Gospel of St. John, particularly
the 11th, 14th and 15th chapters. Again and again,
did I read them to her, at her request. On one occasion,
while reading the 11th, she stopped me at the 36th
verse and exclaimed, ' Jesus wept ! O what compas-
sion ! what love and sympathy ! How delightful !'

" When in severe pain, she groaned and said, ' I want
patience ;' and when engaged in prayer, she would say,
' Pray that I may have patience.' On one occasion,
after reading in the Psalms, she said, ' I feel that God is
with me. O he is precious. Yes : God is my strength
and my refuge.' On another occasion, she turned to me
and said, ' O ! I have had such sweet thoughts of heaven
this morning—all the morning.'

" ' But a few moments before she died, I said, is your
Saviour as precious now, dear Susan, as he has been in
times past ? ' O yes !' was her faint but distinct reply,

'He is precious; the chiefest among ten thousand and altogether lovely!' She soon became speechless, and her eyes seemed fixed. I asked her if she knew me. She quietly turned her eyes upon me with an expression which left no doubt, and the next moment, as I supposed, expired without a groan or struggle.'

"And does this seem to us, my friends, a mysterious and unscrutable disposition, and hard to be reconciled with the goodness and care of a gracious providence? But do we not know that 'He is a God who hideth himself and giveth not account of any of His matters.'

> 'God moves in a mysterious way,
>   His wonders to perform;
> He plants his footsteps in the sea,
>   And rides upon the storm.'

And shall we doubt and hesitate, my brethren, respecting the missionary work, because some fall victims to its dangers? . If those of feebler constitutions sink, is the work, therefore, not of God, or cannot he command the means by which his merciful designs, long since foretold, shall be accomplished in behalf of a perishing, heathen world? Be it far from us to limit the Holy One of Israel, or, in withholding our alms and prayers, forbear our part in aid of the missionary enterprize, because we cannot fathom his councils and interpret all his ways. Did the numrous and trying disasters which attended its early settlement, prevent God's gracious purposes in behalf of our own beloved country, now teeming with an abundant population and all the fruits of civilization and religion? Why, then, should misfortunes discourage us, or bring in doubt the favorable scheme of Providence, touching the moral renovation of other benighted, pagan lands ? We may not, on earth, expect a suspension of the established laws of nature, however able the Almighty is to suspend them, and may do so, whenever it shall be his sovereign pleasure."

The following lines are from the gifted pen of Mrs. Sigourney :

ON THE DEATH OF MRS. SAVAGE, LATE WIFE OF THE REV. DR. SAVAGE,
MISSIONARY AT CAPE PALMAS, AFRICA.

" *What I do, thou knowest not now—but thou shalt know hereafter.*"

Shalt know hereafter !—Father ! wilt thou wait
  In calm submission to thy Master's will ?
Mother !—lamenting o'er thy loved one's fate,
  Say,—canst thou rule thy spirit and be still ?
Sisters and brothers !—sorrowing—will ye take
This promise to your heart, for the Redeemer's sake ?

Shalt know hereafter !—Tender, faithful friend !
  The chosen partner of that heaven-taught breast,
Will this console thee, as thy footsteps tend,
  At mournful evening, to her lowly rest ?
Doth it not gird thee to thy lot of care,
And touch with healing balm, thine agonizing prayer.

Thou know'st not, Afric ! sad of heart and blind,
  Unskilled the precious Book of God to read ;
Thou canst not know, what moved that soul refined,
  Thy lot of wretchedness to heed,
And from her fireside, bright with hallowed glee,
To dare the boisterous surge and deadly clime for thee.

As her loved home, she hailed thy sultry shore,
  Thy dark-browed children to her side she drew,
And sacred music, as a gift, she bore

To lure them upward, where her pleasures grew,
So sweet a song-bird, from her field of air,
Incites her new-fledged train a bolder flight to dare.

Oh Church of God! who on that darkened coast,
    Dost sow thy seed in weariness and pain,
Count not thy mission-labours light, or lost,
    Though clouds should gather, wild with wind and rain.
On! On! Be firm! Thy harvest song shall be—
Praise to the Lord of Hosts, with whom is victory!

CHAPTER VII.

THE stroke by which Mrs. Savage was so soon removed from her chosen work, fell heavily upon her sorrowing survivors. But, upon the over-hanging cloud, the bow of promise shone brightly, and their hearts were cheered by many tokens of God's blessing. The condition of the Mission was, upon the whole, encouraging. A second house had been erected on Mt. Vaughan, and another school house for the separate accommodation of the female department, which was now considerably enlarged. Mr. and Mrs. Perkins passed safely through the acclimating fever, and were soon actively engaged in their new duties. Mr. Payne continued to superintend the boys' school at Mt. Vaughan, and to preach occasionally at Grahway, eight miles east of the Cape, and at Half Cavalla, four miles farther in the same direction. At both these places, schools were established under the superintendence of Mr. Appleby and Mr. Byron.

The Grahway people were proverbially superstitious, even among their countrymen. The following incident will serve as an illustration.

A house had been struck by lightning, which passed
through the roof into the ground floor, tearing up the
earth in its passage. The people immediately conceived
the idea that the thunder had concealed itself, and, unless removed, would cause them continual trouble by attracting other thunder. As no ordinary doctor was skilful enough to bring to light the hidden enemy, application was made to a distinguished member of the craft,
residing at Grand Sesters, about one hundred miles distant. Not being successful in obtaining his services,
they summoned another from the interior. Arrived at
the spot, the great magician commenced his operations.
After employing various incantations, he dug into the
floor to the depth of several feet, when lo! the dreaded
thunderbolt met his gaze in the form of a small piece of
iron ! When he touched the magic thing, to use the
language of the natives, " he died three hours," nor was
he able to leave the spot until forcibly removed.

The situation of Half Cavalla offered such remarkable facilities for usefulness, that the Missionaries early
determined to occupy it as one of their principal stations.
As soon, therefore, as Mr. and Mrs. Perkins were sufficiently recovered from the fever to take part in the labors of the Mission, and Dr. Savage was relieved from
the care and anxiety consequent upon their illness, Mr.
Payne resolved to improve this favorable opening.

On the second of October, he accordingly removed to
Half Cavalla, and, in about a month after, was joined by
his wife.

Here, within a radius of five miles from the Mission
settlement, were twelve towns, all easily accessible, and

though not individually large, containing, collectively, a numerous population. This seemed also the most advantageous point from which to gain access to the interior, being very near the Cavalla River, on the banks of which reside twelve distinct tribes. As the solitary laborer looked abroad over the fields, even then "white unto the harvest," most earnestly did he send home the call for aid.

Alas ! how slow has the Church been to answer the call ! Openings have been made and lost, golden opportunities have been allowed to slip away, and thousands have died in their sins, to rise up in the judgment against us.

Mr. and Mrs. Payne were kindly received by the people, whose frequent intercourse with foreigners had taught them, in some degree, to appreciate both education and the arts of civilized life. Their estimate of the latter was proved by their petitioning Mr. Payne to procure for them a blacksmith's bellows. Their substitute for this was exceedingly rude, but they manifested much skill in the working of iron. Mr. Payne was astonished to find, in a blacksmith's house, a variety of tools, and two gunstocks which he had made, entirely, and put on. Twenty-two pupils attended the day schools ; and fifteen adults, most of whom spoke broken English, came in the evening to receive instruction. We copy the following, as a remarkable example of improvement after two months and a half attendance.

" I want to keep God's laws. My English name is Thomas Wilson—my Grebo name is Gnebur. I want to be a God-man. Then I want to try to make my coun-

4

try people turn to God. But God must help me, before
I can make them turn to Him when I speak to them.
Mr. Payne teaches me to read and spell and write.
Every thing I learn, he teaches me all. I live with
him. He does me good too. I have not time to write
any more now. I want you to pray for me.

THOMAS WILSON."

The Rev. Mr. Minor had sailed from Cape Palmas
early in April. He spent some time in visiting several
positions on the Gold Coast, and reached home in July
following. His visit to the United States was in accordance with the advice of his brethren " for the restoration
of his health, for obtaining priests' orders, and for other
purposes connected with the interests of the Mission."

In February, 1840, he again embarked for Africa,
accompanied by Mrs. Minor and the Rev. Joshua Smith.
They arrived at Cape Palmas early in April, and found
their brethren greatly encouraged by an evident blessing
on their labors.

For several weeks previous, considerable seriousness
had been observed among the scholars at Mt. Vaughan,
and hopes were entertained that nineteen had passed
from death unto life. They who had sown in tears
were now reaping in joy. The prayers of those who had
labored in faith and patience were heard, and " God
had manifested His name" among the heathen. The
power of Divine grace had reached the heathen captive
even in his strong holds of superstition and sin, and now
led him forth, exulting in the glorious liberty of the children of God.

One of the first to yield to this gracious influence, was Susan Savage, already alluded to in the first part of this work. She expressed her feelings in several notes addressed to her teachers and young companions, of which the following is a specimen.

"I take this opportunity to write you a few lines to let you know that I think the Lord has changed my heart, and, I hope, yours too. When I was in my sins I was in such danger, and did not know it till now. If I had died in my sins, where should I have been? I should have been in everlasting punishment. But God was so kind as to spare me. I ought to be thankful for this kindness. He sent His only son to suffer and die on the cross for us, that we might be saved; and I know that we do not deserve it, and if He had not died for us, we should go to hell; and if he had not sent Missionaries, we should never have heard about God."

"SUSAN A. SAVAGE."

Another interesting convert was a boy from a cannibal tribe, about fifty miles distant, who, several months before, had followed Dr. Savage home from a journey, and attached himself to the school. His personal appearance was unusually savage and forbidding, with which his temper seemed to correspond. To use the expression of his companions, he was "bad too much;" but the grace of God transformed him into a meek and humble follower of Christ, as remarkable for docility and mildness, as he had heretofore been for their opposites. Some, no doubt, who professed to profit by this solemn season, mistook the force of example for genuine religious conviction; but others proved their sincerity by a consistent life, and have since died in faith, giving glory to Him who thus brought them out of darkness into his marvellous light. A few yet remain, to testify to the power of that still small voice which quietly, but effectually, broke their fatal slumber.

The influence of this heavenly visitation was felt, in some measure, at Cavalla also. Two or three of the pupils came forward to profess their faith in Christ, and the claims of Christianity began to awaken more atten-tion and interest among the people. Some gave us their opinion, that this " God-palaver," was untrue and un-worthy of regard ; but others said, " Not so—hitherto we have been ignorant of this subject ; thus far it appears to be good ; let us try it before we reject it as good for nothing." The public services on the Sabbath were better attended, and the mirth which they had at first excited, gave place to a becoming seriousness. The use of prayers and hymns in the native language, no doubt contributed much to produce this result.

The following specimens extracted from a small Hymn book prepared by the Rev. Mr. Wilson, and printed at the Missionary press of the A. B. C. F. M. at Cape Palmas, may be interesting to the reader.

> 1. Gnâ woĕ Yisu Kraisĭ yĕ ?
> A wodă yeu, â di bro mah,
> Bâ hă gnebo biyĕ Kuh kwah,
> Yisi Kraisĭ â ne hanhka.

> 2. Gnâ woĕ Yisu Kraisĭ yĕ ?
> Kârĭ â ni ămu hanhka ;
> Ne â mâ ă băyĭtĭme,
> Yisu Kraisĭ â ne hanhka.

3. Gnâ woĕ Yisu Kraisĭ yĕ ?
   A pro a hânâ koh ä ta
   A pĕ nyinâ koh ânm mâh
   Yisu Kraisi a ne hanhka.

4. Gnâ woe Yisu Kraisĭ yĕ ?
   A kwa änm mâh ti biyĕ,
   A ni änm ä plĕ ble ne,
   Yisu kraisĭ â ne kanhka.

1. Who is like Jesus Christ ?
   He came from Heaven to earth,
   To take all people away from devil,
   Jesus Christ is good.

2. Who is like Jesus Christ?
   Because he does us good ;
   And he is our friend,
   Jesus Christ is good.

3. Who is like Jesus Christ ?
   He sold his life for us;
   He paid his blood for us,
   Jesus Christ is good.

4. Who is like Jesus Christ ?
   He follows us every day ;
   He makes our hearts glad.
   Jesus Christ is good.

HEAVEN.

1. Hĕvĕneh ĕh mâ Gnĭsuah tedĕh ;
   Hanh Enje peplândĭ nede ;
   Hanh gnebo nede tĕh nĕnu ;
   Gnebo kuhkwih oh näh mude.

2. Kbŭně kuhkwih eh yede ne ;
   Blidi yidi, kěkrā yidi,
   Swěh yidi kedidá yidi,
   Eh năh dide teděh něnu.

3. Gnono nede Gnïsuah mâh
   Oh năh yi blidi dǐ němā
   Oh plě mi blenu ti biye,
   Kârï oh tih Gnïsuah mâh.

4. Bă nu Gnïsuah winh tětinu,
   Bă ko ne, ä mi nâ yinim ;
   Ne ä miwă nâ mâh nemu,
   Ne ä ple mi blemu băka.

1. Heaven is God's place,
   Many good angels there,
   Good people are there,
   Bad people cannot go there.

2. Wickedness is not there,
   No palaver, no sickness there,
   No poor, no trouble there,
   And all these things cannot go there.

3. Those that live to God
   See no palaver, but
   Their hearts will be glad always,
   Because they live to God.

4. We must keep God's words now ;
   If we die we shall see Him ;
   And we shall live to Him ;
   And our hearts shall be glad much.

It may be here remarked, that the convert from heathenism should never be judged by the same exalted and

rigid standard which we apply to the professor of religion in a Christian country. We must contemplate the one, at the period of his spiritual regeneration, as just emerging from the lowest depths of ignorance and superstition ; while the other, at the same period, is standing upon the high ground of intellectual and moral advancement. In one, the habitual contact with vice, in its most debasing forms, has blunted, and nearly obliterated, the moral perception ; while in the other, the opposite influences have imparted to it the highest degree of acuteness.

We do not marvel then, that the one should regard, as a small and venial fault, that which the more enlightened conscience would condemn as a flagrant sin. The first disciples of Christianity were converted Pagans, and the tone of warning and rebuke in which they are so often addressed by St. Paul, is as applicable now as it was then.

CHAPTER VIII.

THE review of this year (1840) shows it to have been one of great prosperity. The number of pupils at the different stations now exceeded one hundred, all of whom, with few exceptions, had learned to read. Some of the more advanced had commenced the study of grammar, geography, and arithmetic, and four were employed as teachers and interpreters. But it was in the spiritual condition of the Schools, to which reference has been already made, that the most animating encouragement was found.

It was great cause of thankfulness also, that none of the missionaries had been removed by death. Mrs. Minor, though at one time so ill that her life was despaired of, had been mercifully restored. When her attendant physician had abandoned all hope of her recovery, and her sorrowing friends were gathered around her bed to witness her death, an unexpected change took place in her disease, and she was again permitted to resume her labors

4*

Dr. Savage had been induced, by the partial failure of his health, to try the effects of the sea air in a voyage to the Leeward Coast, in which direction it was deemed advisable to prosecute inquiries in reference to future stations ; but had returned in a few months, quite restored. He had been unexpectedly detained on the Gold Coast, no vessel touching there, bound to Cape Palmas, until January, 1841. Much valuable information had, however, been acquired, and at Dix Cove, he had embraced an opportunity of performing missionary duty, by instructing a number of young men, and holding religious services.

In April, 1841, the health of Mrs. Payne became so seriously impaired by her unremitted labors, that a sea voyage was deemed absolutely necessary for its restoration. Her husband, therefore, embarked with her for the United States, where, after four years absence, they arrived safely in July following. This year proved unusually unhealthy, and before its close, Mr. and Mrs. Perkins were also compelled to seek renewed strength in their native land, having previously tried an excursion to Sierra Leone, without effect.

We have already referred to the causes which rendered it desirable to open a station without the boundaries of the colony, and to Mr. Minor's visit to Garraway, with a view to this object. The attempt having failed in that quarter, it was subsequently renewed in an opposite direction, and, in the autumn of 1841, Mr. Minor removed to Taboo, a point on the Leeward Coast about forty miles east of Cape Palmas. About the same time, the school for the children of the colonists was abandoned ;

and Mr. Appleby was removed from Grahway to Rockbookah, the capital of the Baboes, a tribe also beyond
the limits of the colony, These people occupied the territory lying next west of the Plaboes, among whom Mr.
Minor had established himself, thus forming a connecting
link between Cavalla and Taboo.

The Rev. Mr. Smith, who superintended Mr. Payne's
station during his absence, after speaking of the general
prevalence of disease (dysentery) during this year, remarks, that it had elicited new proofs of the superstition of the natives.   He says: "During the sickness
mentioned, I was roused, one morning, early, by a
noise, the cause of which I could not comprehend.
Looking out, I saw men, women, and children, running
towards the woods, shouting and making various noises, and
when they seemed to have reached the end of their race,
the report of two guns was heard. On inquiring into
the matter, I was informed that the doctors had directed
the people to beat their houses with sticks, and chase
the sickness away to the bush."

Having spent six months in making known at home
the wants and success of their mission, Mr. and Mrs.
Payne again embarked for Africa, accompanied by Miss
M. V. Chapin, and Miss Martha D. Coggleshall.

The latter, like Mrs. Savage, was summoned from
her work, almost before it was begun. She had proved
her entire devotion to her Master's service, and he called
her to enter upon her reward. On the 23rd of April
she was seized with the acclimating fever, and died on
the 3rd of May.

Miss Coggleshall was the only daughter of Josiah

Coggleshall, of Bristol, R. I. In the spring of 1830, she went to reside with her grandmother, in Warren, about a mile from the Episcopal Church, then recently established under the pastoral care of the Rev. George W. Hathaway. Although quite a child, she was much interested both in the Church and Sunday School. Of the latter, she immediately became a member, and was remarkable for her regular attendance; the weather, or walking seldom causing her to be absent from its valued privileges, notwithstanding the distance at which she lived. She gave early evidences of piety, which grew and strengthened with her age. ⌐She was baptized on the 29th of April, 1835, and confirmed on the 1st of April following; and the solemn vows thus publicly made, were most faithfully observed. " Her piety," says her pastor, " was characterized by great meekness and simplicity, though deep and fervent, and her desires to do good were most self-sacrificing and untiring. Though young in years, so mature was her piety, that she was requested to become a teacher in the Sunday School; but she meekly declined, preferring to continue a learner."

Miss Coggleshall possessed no brilliant talents, and as her residence in early life had been remote from any school, she had had few facilities for mental improvement; but she had endeavored, as far as possible, to make up the deficiences of her education, by diligent improvement of the limited opportunities which she afterwards enjoyed. It was, however, in the qualities of the heart, that she chiefly excelled. She had drank deeply at the fountain of Divine Wisdom : her thoughts had been elevated, and her affections purified, by intimate communion with the Father of Spirits, and all her conversation bore evidence to her high attainments in the spiritual life. She knew that Christ had given to the members of his Church "gifts, differing one from another," and, with a rare humility and judgment, she chose the sphere of duty for which nature and education had fitted her. Had she lived, her time would have been mainly devoted to the sewing department. The following extract from the *Spirit of Missions*, for Sept., 1842, express the deep sorrow occasioned by her loss.

"Rev. Mr. Payne, speaking of Miss Coggleshall, says: "she died, as she had lived, during our short acquaintance with her, a calm, devoted Christian. Had she lived, she would, no doubt, have been eminently useful in a department of the mission for which she was eminently fitted. But 'God seeth not as man seeth, and should we, *can* we, murmur at His dispensations,' who so surely loves His own cause, and makes 'all things work together for good to them that love Him?'"

The Rev. Dr. Savage remarks: "The Mission feels deeply the loss of Miss Coggleshall. She filled an important place in the female department, and that with much promise. Her desires to do good were so simple, and her views of the way and manner, in such Christian subjection to the experience of others, that we could but anticipate much good to the Mission from her labors. She has left upon the minds of all, a conviction that she was a woman of no ordinary attainments in divine life. The influence of her piety was felt and acknowledged in her short intercourse with the children and

others. It was apparent to all that she daily walked
with God, and had her conversation in heaven. We
view, in her death, *a free-will offering* of herself to
God ; and who shall say that it is not ' well-pleasing
in his sight ?' She has gone, and we doubt not, to a
higher and a nobler sphere of action. May this dispensation be sanctified to us all.'

But sickness and death are not the only, nor, indeed,
the greatest trials, which must be encountered by the
faithful ministers of the Cross in a heathen land. The
indifference and ingratitude of those for whose good he labors, are often sources of far keener suffering, and must,
indeed, entirely dishearten him, if he cannot adopt the
sentiment of the Apostle, " I will willingly spend and be
spent for you, though the more abundantly I love you,
the less I be loved." As an illustration of this kind of
trial, we give the following extract from Mr. Payne's
jonrnal.

"Monday, July 25th. This morning, early, I was
waited upon by a large deputation of the Cavalla people,
including all the head men, who brought me a bullock
as a ' dash.' The occasion of this, was as follows :
On Thursday morning last, on going out of my room in
the morning, I found a deputation of three men, from
the ' sedibo,' or soldiers, in waiting for me. The sedibo include all the young and middle aged men who
have houses. They make laws and palavers, on account of real or pretended offences, and are, in fact, the
government of the country, having the power to act as
they wish. The three men, above-named, told their
errand, rather abruptly, by saying, that ' since I had

been at Cavalla, notwithstanding the soldiers protected
my property, I had never given anything to them.
They had now come, in the name of the soldiers, to ask
for three pieees of cloth. They were going on to enume-
rate many other things, when I interrupted them by
saying, 'if the soldiers were determined to fine or rob
me without any cause, that they must take, not only
what they asked, but all that I had, having the same
right to the whole, as to a part.' Soon after these men
had gone, another deputation came, more pleasant in
their manner than the former, but making the same
demand. To them, I gave, in substance, the same answer, only adding, that I must take this matter to the
head men, to know if I was to be thus subjected to lawless soldiery, or if there was any government in the country. Accordingly, in the afternoon, I convened the old
men in the king's house, and asked them who governed
the country, they, or the soldiers? They replied, with
great promptness, 'we do,' and repelled, indignantly,
any other idea. I then told them of the conduct of the
soldiers. They immediately sent men to inquire of the
soldiers, who were assembled in their house, what they
meant by doing such a thing without consulting them.
Their messenger, however, could get no satisfactory answer, and was treated with much disrespect. After
some consultation amongst the old men, they requested me
to return home, saying, that the matter should be settled in a satisfactory manner.

"Soon after, the king followed me home, and told me
that the soldiers had been induced to 'take their mouths
from the white man.' Still, it was evident from his

manner, and various intimations received from several sources, that the matter had not been fully settled. I heard nothing more of it, however, until the next day. I was then informed that the prime mover of the 'palaver' had actually assembled a number of men, the previous night, on the beach with cutlasses, in order to come and take what they wanted from my house. Providentially, the matter was discovered by the head of the soldiers, who immediately called all together in the 'palaver- house,' where the whole matter was fully discussed. From the report made to me of the proceedings of this meeting, it appears that the great mass of the people were opposed to such proceedings, and the council ended in deciding that the individual who suggested this outrage, should be held responsible for every cent lost on my premises.

" On hearing of this meditated robbery, I expressed, everywhere, my astonishment and indignation, declaring that if I were a ' trade-man,' I should consider it unsafe to remain ; but as I was a ' God-man,' I would not leave, until sent away by the people, or convinced by their conduct, that they were not worthy of having the Gospel preached to them. A re-action now commenced. The matter began to be spoken of as shameful—disgraceful—worthy of punishment ; and soon after, the two ringleaders were fined a cow, bullock, goat, &c., for their crime. The people, on all occasions, expressed shame, and a disposition to repair the injury which had been done me, and the matter terminated in their bringing the bullock this morning, as they expressed it, 'to take away their shame.' "

CHAPTER IX.

ALTHOUGH the Missionaries were thus reminded that the work upon which they had entered must be prosecuted amid many discouragements and trials, they were still favored with many tokens of their Father's mercy and love. One of Mr. Payne's earliest communications after the events which we have just recorded, mentions the success which attended his labors, both in his school and among the people generally. In the former, a spirit of deep religious interest was evidently aroused, and among the adult natives, many were becoming dissatisfied with the superstitions to which they had, hitherto, so tenaciously adhered. Some even went so far as to renounce their greegrees and deliver them into his hands, to be committed to the flames; and a decided improvement was manifest in the more general observance of the Sabbath. Mr. Payne writes: "I have never before felt so much encouraged to go forward in the work of the blessed Saviour, as at the present moment. With six communicants, over whom God hath given me the over sight, an overflowing congregation in one of the busiest seasons of the year, and ten candidates for baptism, I feel that I have abundant cause for gratitude and encouragement."

It may not be uninteresting to present some more particular account of the encouraging circumstances referred to above, as contained in Mr. Payne's journal at the time.

" Sunday, Sept. 26.—I preached to the largest congregation at Grahway, I have ever met there. This morning, I admitted to the Church by baptism, eight of the dear children for whom I have been laboring and praying for some years. Most of these children had been on probation for some months, and all of them, long enough to give good evidence of having been ' born again.' " " Saturday, Sept. 31st : Made my usual visit to the three River Cavalla towns, to-day. At Kablah, had a very interesting discussion in reference to the ' Greegree' system. Most of those present, seemed to be convinced of their vanity, though they were not quite prepared to throw them away at once. I was never before permitted to engage in a discussion in which there was manifested so sincere a disposition on the part of the natives to arrive at the truth. One grave old man, after remarking that he had no greegrees, said that he was in the habit of cooking rice for the devil, and putting it before his door. He enquired of Gnebur if this was right. G. answered with great earnestness, ' You say you have no greegrees. Well ! but leave off also to throw away your rice. If you have children, feed them. Do not give your food to what does not exist. Your departed friends, if it be they you feed, cannot come back. In case they are with God, they do not wish to come. If in hell, they cannot come. Upon this subject, the doctors teach *only lies*. We give our money to them for nothing.' ' You have well said, we give our money to them for nothing,' rejoined the old man. ' This year, when I left my home to cut a rice farm, at the instance of a doctor, I killed a fowl to the devil, to induce him to mind my family during my absence. I had not been gone two days, before my child died. Soon after, I was taken ill. I had then a chest nearly full of plates, of which I gave nearly all to the doctors to cure me, but received no benefit from them. To the last one who offered his services, I replied, that I would give nothing more for this object. I am now well.' "

Under the date of Oct. 21st, 1842, we find the following interesting account of the death of one of the converts. " It was with feelings difficult to be described, that, early on Wednesday morning, I received information from one of our scholars, that Budah, or Peter Van Pelt, was dead. He had left us ten days before, complaining of a sore throat, and swelling in his limbs, from the latter of which, however, he appeared to be recovering. He had been absent somewhat longer than he had anticipated ; and, although his former punctuality made us somewhat uneasy, on this account, we hoped that all was well. In this, however, the information now received, showed we were to be disappointed. He was taken ill on Saturday, and on Tuesday was a corpse !

" The messenger who brought these melancholy tidings, said that he had died at Grand Taboo, some thirty-five miles from here, but was to be buried at his father's place, half that distance. Hoping to be able to reach this latter place by the time the corpse should arrive, I took a canoe, and, in three hours, was at the town of Nimbleh, the father of Budah. On landing, however, I was informed that B. had been buried at Grand Taboo, the previous day. I therefore went on to Mr. Minor's, at the River Taboo, not designing to proceed farther. On arriving there, however, I received three messages from King George, of Grand Taboo, urging me to visit his town. Having concluded to do so, I left Mr. Minor's, after early breakfast, and after passing four other small towns, in two hours reached Grand Taboo. As we were entering the town gate, my guide directed my attention to a grave on the left, which, he said, was Budah's. It was made in civilized style, stood entirely alone, and was surrounded by a fence of sticks about six feet long, and meeting at the top, forming a sort of arch over the grave.

" On entering the town, I was met by King Idebabo, alias George, who has visited England and Sierra Leone, and speaks very good English. He saluted me as his ' very dear friend,' and conducted me into a yard enclosing a number of his houses. Budah's mother is a sister of the king, and in this yard Budah died. A scene now followed, which baffles description. Seated around, in the enclosure. were the bereaved parents of the deceased, with a number of his relatives. Whether in consequence of my approach or not, I do not know, but as I drew near, there was a burst of *such wailing* as could only proceed from those upon whom beams not

one ray of hope beyond the grave. Harrowing, however,
as this was to the feelings, an object was soon presented,
which, for a moment, caused me to forget all else.
Seated on the ground before me, almost naked, was a
gray headed, agonized woman. It was Budah's mother.

"As I took my seat, she poured forth afresh the bitterness of her soul, and throwing her eyes and hands
wildly around her, gave vent to her feelings in words
like these : 'Oh, my son ! my son ! Where are you ?
Your father has come now. Don't you see him ? I
know you do. You are glad now ; you are satisfied ; I
know you are, my son.' While repeating these words,
she dragged herself along on the ground, until she got
quite up to me. And, oh ! as she stared at me, wildly
and hopelessly, how I wished that she had that consolation in her son's death, which his life authorized her
to feel.

"Well aware of the suspicious character of the natives, relative to all deaths which occur, I was not without some anxiety as to my reception by the afflicted
relatives of the deceased. I was not long, however, in
suspense. The father, seating himself by my side, after
assuring me how well he knew my kindness and attachment to his son, added, ' eh ye nah te—Guisnah ah te
nae,' (it—B.'s death—is not your affair, but God's.) He
soon afterwards told me that he would put another of
his sons in Budah's place, as he has done. King George's
son, who had been with me, I was assured, too, should
return. Having returned me thanks in a formal and
particular manner for all my kindness to Budah, and
dashed me a goat and fowl, they added, there was one

request which they must make, namely : that as B. had died there, I would endeavor to procure for them a teacher. The king now requested me to write something on a board, descriptive of the character of the deceased, to be placed over his grave. I told him that a board would rot so soon, as to render it useless to put one there, and that a piece of stone would be much better— little expecting to get a suitable one. Very soon, however, he brought me a tablet of soft stone, about eighteen inches in diameter, upon which I wrote with my penknife as follows :

' PETER VAN PELT,

' The son of Sebueh Nimbleh and Badeh, of the Babo tribe. Born 1822. Entered the P. E. Mission School, Cape Palmas, 1837 ; was baptized 1841 ; taught in the Mission School at Cavalla, where he led a godly life, until October 18th, 1842, when, on a visit to this place, he died.'

" Having finished this, Nimbleh, the king of a neighboring town, who had also visited England, asked if I would not read the Burial Service. Ashamed, that the hurry in which I left Mr. Minor's, should have caused me to lose sight of a duty of which I was now reminded by a heathen king, I sent back in haste for a Prayer Book, that I might comply with the request. Soon after dinner, I called the people together, and preached to them ' Jesus and the resurrection.' Before preaching, I sung, as usual, a hymn in Grebo, in which the king and many present, joined at the top of their voices ; and after we had done, the king added, ' thank the Lord.' He expressed his assent, also, to what was said, and only regretted that, having no teacher, they were liable to forget what they now heard. Now, although it was evident to one acquainted with the deceitfulness of the African character, that much of this was said for effect, yet it was interesting to hear such sentiments expressed, where the Gospel was now preached for the first time, and by a people whose character is regarded as peculiarly bad. At 3 o'clock P. M. I read the Burial Service over our dear departed pupil and brother in Christ, and returned to Mr. Minor's. In the Christian character of the youth of whom we have been so unexpectedly deprived, the greatest confidence was reposed by all who knew him. Having been in the Mission from its origin, his mild and amiable deportment had secured for him the favor of all his teachers, before he made a public profession of faith. This was much increased by his godly walk after his admission to the Church."

CHAPTER X.

HE who has always associated with death the glorious hope of life and immortality brought to life in the gospel, can form little idea of the hopelessness and gloom in which the grave is shrouded to the heathen mind. The belief in a future existence is, indeed, prevalent among the natives of West Africa, but of the nature of that existence, they seem to have no definite conception. When questioned as to the destiny of the soul after death, some reply, that it has gone to " Gnisuah," or God ; others, that it has departed to " Kuhblih," or the spirit's land, from whence they expect it to return again, at some indefinite period, in the body of a new born infant. Yet, while assigning to the disembodied soul a residence in some far off and shadowy realm, beyond the grave, or giving to their children the names of deceased relatives, whose spirits they suppose to have thus reappeared on earth, they have many rites and ceremonies which would seem to recognize their presence in the place of burial, or, as still separate spiritual existences, attending them in their daily haunts of life. The grave yard is never entered without dread and trembling, and on great occasions, when the dead are invoked as witnesses of some public deed, the speaker turns his face towards the resting place of the sleeping dust, as he calls upon the spirit to listen and observe.

The dead are supposed to exert great influence, either for good or evil, upon surviving friends or enemies, and hence, are frequently addressed in the most solemn denials of all past ill will, and the warmest assurances of affection and esteem.

The desire to propitiate their good will is evinced in numberless superstitious observances, such as offering to them a portion of the daily meal, carrying food or fire to the grave, &c.

At the time of burial, the corpse is laid out in the state suited to his wealth and rank. If a person of consequence, he will probably be stretched upon a rude bier, covered with cloths of various kinds and colors, and overhung with a canopy of the same materials. The body is painted in every fantastic variety of figure and hue, and adorned with all the scraps of finery which can be collected for the occasion. Rings and beads are strung upon the neck, arms, and limbs, and sometimes, a number of looking glasses are laid about the body, as if to gratify him with the view of the display. The chests containing his various possessions in cloth, tobacco, crockery, cooking utensils, &c., are brought out, to impress the beholder with a due sense of his wealth and importance, and some of all these articles are deposited with him at the grave, for his use in another world. A bullock is killed in sacrifice to the devil, and the corpse, with the cloth, &c., sprinkled with the blood. The body is either buried beneath the ground, or laid upon the surface, with a canoe turned over it.

The African frequently expresses his feelings at the death of a relative in the significant phrase, "my heart burns," and, no doubt, resentment is often the predominant emotion. Except in the case of infancy or extreme old age, he recognizes no other cause of death than witchcraft, and believing himself robbed of his friend through the malign influence of some enemy, it is not strange that he is angry, as well as grieved. Of course his first wish is revenge. How is the guilty one to be discovered? Perhaps some individual is known to have borne ill will to the deceased, or the "doctor" has privately designated the murderer. Sometimes, as the canoe containing the body is carried along in the funeral procession, the bearers come to a full stand, or turn backwards, declaring that the deceased refuses to be carried to his grave. Winding about in a devious and zigzag track, they again resume their passage to the place of burial, but presently, the corpse impels them against a house, which is immediately marked as the dwelling of the murderer! The doomed resident knows well what now awaits him. The poisonous Sassa Wood must prove his innocence, or lay him low in death. If it prove fatal, his death is hailed as the deserved punishment of his crime; a hole is scooped in the sand, and the body hastily interred, denied a place in the burying ground of his people.

The administration of the Sassa Wood is, no doubt, often to be regarded in the same light as the public execution of a criminal; but there can be no question that

5

it is frequently made the means of gratifying a private revenge. The accusation of witchcraft is the most certain means of removing an individual whose wealth has excited the jealousy of his neighbors, or who has otherwise become obnoxious to public or private resentment.

Hundreds are annually sacrificed to this dreadful custom, and there is reason to believe, from the powerful narcotic influence of the drug, that many are interred, whose life is not extinct. The Missionary may sometimes succeed in rescuing the victim from the rage of popular violence, but he does not, therefore, necessarily secure his safety. Unwilling to live under the odium of a suspected wizard, he will voluntarily subject himself to the ordeal; but he gains an important advantage if some more deadly ingredient is not mingled in the draught by his infuriated enemies.

In Mr. Payne's journal, a few weeks later, we find a singular illustration of the puerile and debasing superstitions of the Grahwayans. He had gone on the Sabbath, to one of their towns to preach, as usual; but on his arrival, he received a message from the head men, requesting that the service might be omitted, as the people were all engaged in making an offering to the devil. The occasion was as follows:

Several months before, a very successful fisherman had killed a large fish at sea, which the doctors said was the Devil's child, and, of course, had greatly excited the wrath of the Evil Spirit. In order to appease this dreaded being, the unfortunate man was ordered to leave the town for a specified time, but venturing to to return before the allotted period, he was overtaken by the devil's vengeance and drowned. But still, the offence was not sufficiently punished. The devil was angry with all the people of the town, and would not suffer them to catch any fish; and being told that a bullock would appease him, they were now offering the required sacrifice.

On another occasion, Mr. Payne mentions his having found the same people in a state of great excitement on account of the death of a child, from an accidental blow from the cutlass of his step-father. He writes: " No accident seems, in such cases, to be recognized by this people. The man who has the misfortune to kill another in this manner, is obliged to flee from his country immediately, never to reside in it again; the popular belief being, that in case he should, it would never cease raining. The author of the accident above, fled as soon as it was done ; and when I arrived, not a vestige of his house remained. It had been pulled down instantly, thrown into the sea, and its very foundation so entirely removed, as scarcely to leave a trace of its ever having supported a house. The enraged populace had already killed three bullocks belonging to the family of the unfortunate man, and were, at the moment of my reaching the place, quarrelling about others.

" There is a singular circumstance connected with the burial of persons killed in this manner. They are not placed in, or on the ground, as in other cases ; but, after being bandaged up in a part of a canoe, they are taken to a particular tree, against which they are placed in a standing position. They are surrounded, however, by pieces of timber, to protect them from leopards or

other beasts of prey. The reason of this singular custom, I have not ascertained."

On the eleventh of February, 1843, the Mission received an accession in the arrival of the Rev. Samuel Ha-
zelhurst of Philadelphia, who was located at Mt. Vaughan.
The Rev. Mr. Smith had resumed the care of the station
at the river Cavalla, and the Rev. Mr. Minor was successfully prosecuting his labors at Taboo. At the termination of the first year after his return from America, Mr.
Payne was able to present the following gratifying report
of his labors, a sufficient proof that the white man may
accomplish much, even in that debilitating and sickly
land.

" SUNDAY, April 2d, 1843.

" It is one year, to-day, since I re-entered upon the
duties of this station, after returning from America.
During this time, I have preached here every Sunday
morning except one, when I preached the annual sermon
before the Mission at Mt. Vaughan. Besides preaching
on Sunday, and giving daily religious instruction to the
boarding scholars connected with the station, I have
also preached, in most instances nine, on an average
six times during the week, in the villages around Cavalla,
making a total of three hundred and twelve discourses
during the year, besides translating two hours in the
morning, and attending to the multifarious duties connected with the charge of a large family. I have not
been prevented, in one instance, that I can recall, from
discharging my duties, by indisposition."

Mr. Payne had made it a permanent object to reduce
and acquire the Grebo tongue, and had so far succeeded

as to be able to assist in translating the Gospel of St. Mark, before his visit to America. After his return, he devoted his attention principally to the Prayer Book, and, at the period of which we are now writing, had translated the Morning and Evening Service, Occasional Prayers, Selections of Psalms, and the Psalter, to the fortieth Psalm. A part of the Morning Service, with the Commandments, was read every Sabbath in public, besides other suitable prayers and hymns.

CHAPTER XI.

Death of Mrs. Maria V. Savage—Parentage, birth, and early life—Determination to offer her services for Africa—Letter to the Rev. Dr. Vaughan—Farewell letter to her friends—Voyage and arrival in Africa.

Our next record must repeat the story of sickness and bereavement. Miss Maria V. Chapin had passed through the acclimating fever with little suffering, and had entered upon the labors of missionary life with the highest promise of extensive usefulness. On the 2d of June, 1842, she was united in marriage with the Rev. Dr Savage, and continued to discharge her important duties with great zeal and ability, until she was seized with her last illness. She died at Mt. Vaughan, December 23d, 1843, aged twenty-three years.

Miss Chapin was the daughter of Mr. Consider Chapin, and was born in Derby, Vermont. When about sixteen years old, she entered the Female Academy at Burlington, where she was first impressed with the claims of Divine truth, and devoted herself to the service of her Redeemer. She was subsequently employed for two years in the vicinity of Topsham, in her native state; but believing that a warmer climate would be more favorable to her health, she determined to seek a situation as governess in one of the southern states. With this design, she wished to add to her other qualifications a knowledge of music; and being unwilling that her father should incur the expense of her instruction, she entered one of the mills at Lowell, and with the profits of her industry, engaged a teacher, and devoted her leisure time to the acquisition of this accomplishment. But God had another place for her. " A man's heart deviseth his way, but the Lord directeth his steps." In the autumn of 1841, she attended an evening lecture, in which the Rev. Mr. Payne gave an account of his labors in Africa, and presented a strong appeal in behalf of the dying heathen of that benighted continent. Her sympathies were strongly enlisted, and the inquiry immediately presented itself, "why should not I give myself to this work." Seriously and prayerfully she pondered the question of duty, and after consulting her pastor, determined to offer her services to the Foreign Committee. The following communication to the Rev. Dr. Vaughan, then secretary of that body, will show with what feelings she looked forward to the work.

" The question of my personally engaging in a Mission to the Heathen, has long been before my mind, and received, as it claimed, my most serious and prayerful consideration. This great work is now brought nearer to my mind than I could ever before regard it, and I trust it does not appear the less desirable. I have considered the subject in every light, so far as I am able from the information I have respecting it, and I can never take up the question again, to find reasons for going. My mind is now settled as to the duty, should no unforeseen

providence prevent, of leaving home and country for a
heathen land. A long adieu to my kindred and friends
will rend the heart ; I feel already that it will ; but at
the same time, the prospect of doing good to some poor
heathen soul will fill it with joy, and the hope of advancing, in ever so small a degree, the cause of my Redeemer, will be a constant feast to the soul. The silent
tear of parental affection and solicitude would indeed
overpower me, had I not confidence that He who thus
afflicts, will support, my beloved parents. Neither, in
the present case, can I think it proper to follow, altogether, the opinion of friends. With the smiles of my
heavenly Father, I must be happy, though friends forsake me. I feel an inexpressible pleasure in commending
them to God, assured that they will be enabled to give
up their child without regret, in the hope that she will
do good to perishing souls. And I have, also, that blessed hope, that, should we never again meet in this world,
we shall be a happy family circle at the right hand of
God. Still, I feel my own insufficiency to decide a
question of such importance as that of leaving all that
the heart holds most dear on earth, to encounter the
toils and hardships of a missionary life. Indeed, I
would not decide for myself. I trust solely to Him
who has promised grace and strength. Though, at
times, great weakness has constrained me to shrink
at the prospect before me, I have been consoled and
supported in the assurance that God will perfect
strength in my weakness. I feel a desire to act in
accordance with the will of God ; to do nothing
which would be displeasing in His sight. I think I am

willing to be, and to do, anything for the sake of the
glory of God ; and if I can only be sure that I am wholly
under the guidance of His spirit, I shall be fully satisfied. It is difficult, I know, to analyze one's feelings,
and ascertain the real character of the motives by which
we are actuated ; I feel my liability to be deceived, and
my need of Divine assistance. The only question which
concerns me, is, are my motives pure and holy ? Never
would I bear the missionary standard, without having in
my heart the missionary spirit. I have calmly and deliberately weighed the subject, and feel, that no attrac-
tion from its novelty, no impulse from its moral dignity,
can bear up, and carry forward any one, amidst the
long continued labors of almost uniform sameness which
you represented to me ; nothing but a thorough conviction of being in the path of duty, nothing but the ap-
proving smile of heaven, can keep one from despondency,
from sinking into hopeless inactivity ; but I have calmly
and deliberately weighed the subject, and feel a willingness to give up comforts, and submit to privations, to
forsake ease and endure toil, to assemble no more ' with
the great congregation,' but seek the Lord in the wilderness, or in the desert—in short, to make every sacrifice
of personal ease and gratification, for the one great object of making known a crucified Saviour to those who
are perishing in ignorance and sin. Indeed, what sacrifice can be too great, if what is done for Him who
bought us with his own blood can be called a sacrifice,
for those to make, who have themselves experienced the
efficacy of a Saviour's blood ? I have reflected, that
should I go out, cheered by the smiles of friends, and en-

5*

couraged by the approbation of the churches, yet soon,
amidst a people of strange speech, I shall see these smiles
only in remembrance, and hear the voice of encouragement only in dying whispers across the ocean. Yet,
when I have considered the command of Christ, 'Go
ye and teach all nations,'—and when, in pouring out my
soul on this subject to the Father of light, I have
realized more of that sweet 'peace which passeth all
understanding ;' objections have all dwindled to a point ;
I have been enabled, by the eye of faith, to discover the
finger of God, pointing me to the benighted African, and
have heard his voice saying, with the affection of a
Father and the authority of a Sovereign, 'Come, follow
me'—' He that loveth father or mother more than me is
not worthy of me ;' and adding, for my encouragement,
' I will never leave thee nor forsake thee.' I do feel that
God calls me to become a missionary, and do, with this
belief, resolve to consider myself as devoted to that service, hoping that God will qualify me, and make me a
faithful servant for Christ's sake."

As has been before stated, Miss Chapin embarked
for Africa, in company with Mr. and Mrs. Payne, January 28th, 1842. Her farewell letter to her friends,
closed on board the vessel, expresses her satisfaction on
the prospect of soon being on missionary ground, but
shows that she felt deeply, the pain of parting from her
friends. " Do not think," she writes, " that I can bid
adieu to the shores of America without a tear—no ; I
cannot ! The separation is far more trying than I had
anticipated ; but I must not indulge myself in saying
what is in my heart. Nature struggles hard, and I stop

to wipe away the tears which gather fast, and interrupt the traces of my pen,—still, I go willingly, cheerfully."

The vessel encountered much boisterous weather, and the passengers suffered much from sea-sickness. In thirty days they anchored at Sierra Leone, and afterward visited Monrovia ; but Miss Chapin's letters contain only passing notices of these places. On the twenty-sixth of March, she thus records, in her journal, her feelings on arriving at her future home. " Yesterday, at half-past eleven, we anchored at Cape Palmas. Dined with the Rev. Mr. Wilson, Missionary of the American Board, and there met Dr. Savage, who accompanied us to Mt. Vaughan. Never shall I forget my emotions when my eyes first rested on the spot which had been the home of those faithful servants of God, for whom I had offered so many prayers; and found myself surrounded by those degraded beings, whom I hoped to be the happy, though unworthy instrument, of turning from the error of their ways, and of leading to the cross of Christ. Oh, my God ! qualify me for my work ; make me a faithful servant in thy cause. Though I be called to suffer, may I have grace to bear it all with patience, ever bearing in mind what Christ suffered to save me, one of the vilest of sinners, from the torments of hell."

CHAPTER XII.

Mrs. Savage's Illness—Extracts from her Letters and Journal.

SHE was confined to her room, by the acclimating fever, only twelve days, and soon after her recovery, writes to her parents: "I feel an entire confidence that I am in the path of duty, and give you my assurance that I am contented and happy." Referring to the new relation into which she was about to enter, she thus writes: "God grant that I may have a full sense of the responsibilities I am bringing upon myself, and grace to meet every difficulty. Guide and direct me, oh my Father! in all the duties which may subsequently devolve upon me. I still feel, at times, that I am not qualified for the duties devolving upon the wife of a missionary, but am much encouraged by the promise, 'my grace is sufficient for thee.' I have resolved, by the assistance of God, that I will be a dutiful and affectionate wife, and endeavor, both by precept and example, so to govern all pertaining to my household, that we may in truth say: 'As for me and my house, we will serve the Lord.' As I look around upon this dark land, and see so many sinking in ignorance and sin, I am led to cry out, 'Lord! what wilt thou have me to do,' and what am I doing? what have I this day done, to advance the cause of my dear Redeemer? What has my conversation and conduct been? has it been such that others would take knowledge of me, that I had been with Jesus? God grant that the coming day may be more wholly consecrated."

She had now assumed the superintendance of the girls' school at Mt. Vaughan, and was actively engaged in efforts for the salvation of the people around her, both colonists and natives. With what ardor she engaged in these labors of love, and with what diligence and fidelity she watched over her own spiritual interests, is evidenced by her journal.

" June 14th—This day has been one of much prayer for the salvation of these miserable people. I now see one great reason why Christians are not more interested for them. If they would inform themselves more respecting them,—of their depravity and wretchedness, they would wake up to a sense of their duty."

"June 20th—Have this evening been led to reflect much upon death, partly from visiting the graves of those who have fallen a sacrifiee (a willing one) to this sultry clime. O glorious death! to be counted worthy to suffer and die for him, who shed his blood so freely for our sins. Have felt, at times, that it would be a severe trial to leave these people, thus degraded and in need of instruction, to lie down in the grave ; but I fear that it is because I am not willing to depart. Oh, merciful God ! lead me to give up myself more entirely into thy hands, that I may be willing to live and labor, or to suffer and die, as thou dost think best ; make me truly thine !"

" June 22d—This day, have had much spiritual enjoyment. We hoped that there was some prospect of an
awakening among the children; but the night has
brought with it a severe disappointment. One of our
boys, and sad to tell, one who was a communicant in
our Church, has fallen into gross sin. Oh, God! grant
that it may make me more watchful and more faithful
in the performance of my duties. Let me not be discouraged, but labor and pray, relying upon thy precious
promise that, 'in due season we shall reap if we faint
not.' Help me, oh, God! to be more faithful, and give
me a more ardent love for the souls of those around me;
but forbid that I should forget to work out my own salvation with fear and trembling."

" June 29th.—This day has been observed by us,
as one of fasting and prayer, for the blessing of God
upon our Mission. Have visited and prayed with three
of our communicants, who give evidence of vital piety.
Many prayers have been this day offered, for an awakening among us, who are Christians, and many more
for these benighted people. May God hear and answer
them. May we, from this time, be stimulated to greater
effort in saving souls. We see, before our eyes, the
eternal danger of souls 'living without hope and without God in the world,' and may an energy, now dormant, be waked up, which shall spare no pains, and
stop at no difficulties, till the Gospel of Jesus Christ
which alone can bring 'life and immortality to light,'
shall have cast its reviving beams upon this dark habi-
tation of the earth, now filled with cruelty and crime.
May we not be deterred by danger, or discouraged by

disappointment and trials, but labor faithfully in the cause of our blessed Redeemer, relying upon his promise for a blessing."

"June 30th.—Have been engaged to-day in visiting, with the children, the colonists around us. Some seem to feel an interest for the salvation of their souls, while others, who profess to know and serve the Lord, do not know what is to save them, but seem to rely upon the few outward forms which they have "

"August 10th.—This day has been one of doubt and darkness. Have felt a depression of spirits, yet know not why. It is not that God has withdrawn his blessings, for they are pouring upon me innumerably. A kind and affectionate husband is one of the chief blessings of my life. Every temporal blessing necessary for my comfort, God, in his goodness, has bestowed upon me. He even allows me the blessed privilege of laboring in his cause. O! that I might be a more faithful servant! Wake up, my soul! to a sense of thy duty; no longer let thy powers lie dormant, while souls are fast sinking to endless death! Forgive this coldness, oh my God! and help me, from this time, to live more to thee—even wholly to thee. May I act under the habitual and uniform impulse of love to my exalted Saviour, and oh, God! grant that I may, with reason, adopt the exulting declaration of the prophet:—'Although the fig tree shall not blossom, neither shall fruit be in the vine; the labor of the olive shall fail, and the fields shall yield no meat; the flock shall be cut off from the fold, and there shall be no herd in the stall; yet will I rejoice in the Lord; I will joy in the God of my salvation.' "

"August 20th.—I am now brought to the close of another week, and how has it been? What report has it borne to the dread tribunal before which I must soon appear? What has been my occupation, my temper, my conversation, and the state of my heart? Have I suffered my time to pass away with no profit to myself, or to these degraded people amongst whom I dwell? Have I borne with Christian patience and resignation, all the little trials and disappointments I have been called to meet? Alas! my own conscience condemns me for the mis-use of the talents which God has committed to me. Sorrows have not been borne with that submission to the will of God which should characterize every true follower of Christ. I pray God to forgive my murmuring, complaining temper, and to help me to meet all the disappointments, which must attend one in this heathen land, as coming from the All-wise disposer of events. May mercies unnumbered, surrounding me, excite in me the grateful affections to the Giver of all good. As I review the past week, I see much room for improvement. Wilt thou, oh! my God! help me to commence the approaching one in thy fear, and to spend it in thy service. I now resolve, with Divine assistance, to live more devoted to the service of my Redeemer, and to labor faithfully for these souls, relying entirely upon God for a blessing upon my labors."

"August 22d.—This day has been one of trials of the body, which I fear have not been borne with as much Christian patience as they ought to have been. I well know my sufferings are no more than I need, and not half I deserve. But oh! how blessed am I in having the consolations of the Gospel to comfort me, when tried and afflicted! Though the head be weary and the heart be troubled, in my Bible I can find a cure for every ill. Here I can read of that land where sorrow never comes. Privileged indeed, am I, above these people amongst whom I dwell. They too can feel and suffer. Their hearts may sink as low, and ache as bitterly as mine; and yet, the Gospel speaks no peace to them. Oh, my God! wilt thou assist me in teaching them the way of life!"

"August 28th,—Another holy Sabbath is drawing to a close; perhaps the last one I shall spend upon earth. Perhaps, ere another Sabbath shall have dawned on this benighted land, I shall be called to lie down in the grave, there to repose till the last trumpet shall call me to stand before the throne of that Great Being, whom I have, this day, professed to worship. I have been prevented from attending upon the services of His sanctuary, but have had much joy in looking forward to that home which remains for the people of God. Oh, Lord! prepare me to enter into that rest, and even this week, should I become a prey to the 'fell destroyer,' make me ready to depart. Help me so to live, that, when tried and afflicted, I may look forward with joy to my rest in heaven."

CHAPTER XIII.

Account of Mrs. Savage's Last Illness and Death.

THE following account of the last hours of Mrs. Savage. is extracted from a letter addressed, by her husband, to her afflicted relatives in the United States.

"The health of Mrs. Savage had been precarious for a month previous to her decease, generally bad. Her last attack, it may be said, began on the evening of Friday, the 15th of December. She was then in a state of great debility. She continued to the 19th, without much change for the better or worse; at this date, I began to take notes of her case and state of mind.

"On the 19th, as I approached her bedside, she took my hand in the most affectionate manner, and, with a heavenly expression on her countenance, said: 'Yesterday I thought it would be sweet to live, and it appeared to me hard to die; but *not so now*—it will be all for the best.' Towards evening, she desired me to read to her in the Bible, before a disposition to sleep should come on. I took up her own Bible, a book which had been, from the first, her almost constant companion, and read the greater part of the 8th chapter of Romans, the 16th, 17th, 31st, 32d, 38th, and 39th verses, of which I found she had marked. She ex-

pressed great pleasure during the exercise, and appeared
to be greatly comforted. She seemed to suffer less
from pain on the night of the 19th than during the day,
and, except the debility, her symptoms, during the
20th, were more favorable. At about three in the
morning, a severe paroxysm of pain supervened, and her
observation was, 'If I cannot soon find relief, I must
die.' At the height of it, she uttered an exclamation
significant of her sufferings, but the next moment her
voice was raised in a song of praise :

> 'The spirit, in our hearts,
> Is whispering, sinner, come!
> The bride, the Church of Christ proclaims
> To all his children, come!'

"The tune to which she sang it, was Olney. In
the stillness of that moment—the time—the dead hour
of night—in the chamber of sickness and suffering—nay,
as I then began to fear, of death—when her frail body
was racked with pain—the effect was indescribable. It
seemed almost the voice of a sister spirit calling her
upward. And this was the habit of her mind. It was
no effort for her to fix her mind on Christ. Fearful
lest a murmur or a feeling of impatience might arise,
she turns her inward eye upon Him, and in view of
what He had suffered for her, and of the freeness of
His grace and promises, she embraces Him, and He
turns her groans into a song of praise!

"The passion of Christ was her favorite theme.
When questioned by me as to her symptoms, and if in
pain, she would give a suitable answer, but in immediate connection say :—'But oh! how much did the Sa-

viour suffer for us! and shall I shrink from these light
pains? How cheerfully ought I to suffer for Him!'
Perhaps an entry, which I have since found in her
journal, will be properly introduced here.

"September 13th.—Have been ill for three days
past, but am much better, for which I ought to be
thankful to God. I am just beginning to realise that
the missionary must be tried in body and mind. We
must here meet with trials, disappointments, discouragements, and much tribulation; and oh, that I might
amid all these, bear in mind how much more Christ
has suffered for me! When I think of the sufferings the blessed Jesus endured for me, not only in his
body, but his soul;—when I reflect on his agony in the
garden and on the cross, that he suffered the fierceness
of the wrath of the Almighty for me, a sinner, shall I
not bear any thing he is pleased to lay upon me, without a murmur, particularly if, while afflicting the body,
he comforts the soul. God has thus far enabled me to
trust in his promises and apply them to myself, and, ' as
my day, so shall my strength be.' If I am called to great
trials, I trust God will give me great grace to endure
them; if to great duties, great grace to perform them.
I am principally anxious that I may never murmur or
find fault with His dispensations towards me, but glorify
Him at all times, and always be able to say, from the
heart, ' good is the will of the Lord—all his ways are
perfect.' I pray thee oh, my God! to silence every murmur,
and sanctify every light affliction to the good of my soul.
Lord! I have come to thee again and again, and I do
now come to thee for guidance and direction. O, wilt

thou assist me to do thy will, and to be a faithful servant in thy cause, that, when called to give an account
of my stewardship, I may receive, from my Lord, the
happy plaudit, 'well done my good and faithful servant.'
I know I can do nothing of myself, and wilt thou oh, God!
unworthy as I am, assist me by thy grace? O, guide
and direct me in the path of duty, and may it ever be
the motto of my life, ' Lord, *what* wilt thou have me to
do?' "

" During Wednesday night, the twenty-first, she was
restless. Since the last paroxysm of pain mentioned,
she expressed herself to the hour of death, perfectly free
from suffering of any kind. She remarked that she had
much to say, but supposed she ought not to say it, being
so weak. I asked if her Saviour continued to be as near
and dear to her, as she had before found him to be. She
replied : ' O yes ! I think I never really knew before how
precious he is.' Perceiving my emotion, she asked if I
thought she could recover, and begged I would not hesitate to tell her freely. To my reply, she answered :
' Well! as the Lord wills. I am perfectly resigned to
die or live, as He may think best.' And such, it seems
to me, has been the habit of her mind, ever since I first
knew her. In respect to God, she appeared like an affectionate, confiding and obedient child, in the arms of
her Parent, knowing no will but His. It has been a
fixed principle with her, to watch the dealings of God,
to study closely into His Providence, believing that all
He does, is done as a kind Father, disciplining and deal-
ing with His children for their best good."

" The following stanza, which I find written upon a

blank leaf of her Bible, bearing the date of 15th of May,
is illustrative of this."

> "For me, O Lord! whatever lot
> The hours, commissioned, bring ;
> If all my withering blessings die,
> Or fairer clusters spring,
> Grant, Lord! that still, with grateful heart,
> My years resigned may run ;
> 'Tis thine to give or to resume—
> Thy will, not mine, be done."

"Having been called away from her bedside for a
short time, on my return I asked if she had been comfortable. 'Not comfortable in mind,' was her reply.
'What is the matter ?' 'I have been thinking of the natives.' Supposing that, through bodily weakness, she
might have conceived some fear of them, though I never
knew her to manifest the slightest, on any occasion, I
said, 'I would not think of them. Fix your thoughts on
Christ and heaven, and that will draw them off.' 'It
was in that connexion I was thinking of them,' said she,
in an emphatic manner. Her sympathies have ever been
strong in their behalf, and whenever she has witnessed
their customs, so strongly indicative of their degradation,
she has exclaimed, with deep feeling. 'O! could Christians at home but realize their obligations ! how many of
these poor beings would be saved who will soon be lost !'
The salvation of the heathen occupied her waking and
sleeping thoughts. In the dead of night, and when
asleep, has she audibly prayed for the children under
her care, and the last entry made in her journal is that of
a prayer for them. It has been my practice to hold a

prayer meeting on Saturday night, when the older scholars and members of the Mission repeat a verse of Scripture, from memory, upon which I ask questions and give
explanations. Mrs. Savage has often expressed her enjoyment in these meetings, and it is respecting one of
them that she speaks in this extract."

"Am prevented, by indisposition, from attending our
Saturday evening meeting, which I have always enjoyed
when present. O my God! be pleased to sanctify the
instruction now given to the heathen children, here collected. Oh wilt thou dispose the hearts of some of them,
to devote themselves to thy service, and, from this little
school, send forth some, through the length and breadth
of this land, to proclaim Jesus Christ and Him crucified
to the millions of their perishing countrymen."

"As the day broke on the morning of the twenty-
third, and the light shone into the room, the evidence
was too strong, in her countenance, that she was rapidly
sinking into the grave. She had, at about half-past
four, lost all consciousness, and at five, or a little after,
went into convulsions. She afterwards somewhat revived, and though unable to speak, was evidently con-
scious, and aware of her state. Whenever spoken to,
she would turn her suffused eye towards the speaker,
and when asked if her Saviour was near—if all were
peace—it was immediately raised towards heaven, and
the expression that lighted up her countenance, told
more plainly than words could tell, that heaven was her
home. In the afternoon, Mrs. Payne arrived from Cavalla. They had not met for several weeks, and if an
earthly desire remained to be gratified, it was to see this

much loved sister. I shall never forget her countenance
when, leading Mrs. Payne to her bedside, I said, 'My
dear ! here is Mrs. Payne, that dear friend you have so
much desired to see.' She could not speak, nor could she
see ; yet the movement of her lips, the eye and the light
of her countenance, bespoke an intercourse of soul that
told how sweet is the communion of saints, even on
earth."

"She had a third convulsion towards evening, of
much less severity than the former, after which she
rapidly declined, and breathed her last almost in coincidence with the setting of the sun."

Although the deaths of three of our African Missionaries, following each other in such quick succession,
must be regarded as most afflictive proof of the danger to
be incurred in this perilous field, a calm review of the
history of the Mission affords no ground for discourage-
ment. The Church had commenced the enterprise with
a full knowledge of the formidable obstacles which must
oppose its progress. Those who had entered upon the
work, knew well that disease and death lay in their
path, but the command of the Saviour—'Go ye into
all the world and preach the Gospel to every creature,'
was imperative, and admitted of no exception. Looking
upon the perishing millions in the wild wastes of Africa,
for whom Christ had died no less than for the dwellers
in more favored climes, they esteemed it a blessed privilege to encounter any dangers and endure any suffering,
that they might hold up the lamp of life in a region
where brooded the very blackness of moral death. None
counted their lives dear unto themselves, and those who

had been called to lay them down, did so, rejoicing that they were counted worthy to have done the smallest service in this hallowed cause.

Said the first, as her eye was fixed on heaven, then opening before her, " I have no regret that I engaged in this cause. I never experienced so much happiness before, and I die with the assurance that I am in the path of duty."

Said the second, to a friend by her side, " the happiness of living and laboring in this benighted land, will be yours—but I must die. Tell my friends in America that I feel no regret for coming to Africa ;" and then, with an audible prayer for the success of the Mission, she calmly expired in the arms of her Saviour.

Said the third, " I have the assurance that I have been directed by the Lord. I could have wished to live longer, that I might do more for this degraded people, but the will of the Lord be done.'

Those who yet survived, though sorrowing, yet always rejoicing—cast down, but not destroyed—gratefully acknowledged that their loss had been less than might have been reasonably expected. Six years had now elapsed since the establishment of the Mission, during which twelve white laborers had been employed. Of these, three had, indeed, been removed by death, but this was a small proportion in a climate so unfavorable. Six Stations had been opened, operating upon a population of twenty thousand, and imparting instruction to about two hundred persons, men, women and children, in day and evening schools. Thirty persons had been admitted to the Church, of whom more than half were natives.

CHAPTER XIV.

Death of Rev. L. B. Minor—His birth and boyhood—College life—Characteristic incidents.

WE come now to the period of melancholy interest, when the Church was called to mourn the loss of the first clergyman who had fallen in her missionary ranks. On the 29th of May, the African Mission was again most deeply afflicted in the death of the Rev. L. B. Minor, who, among the first to offer for the Foreign Service, had, for six years, devoted himself, with untiring energy and zeal to the cause of Christ in one of its most laborious fields. We have hitherto, only briefly noticed Mr. Minor's labors in connection with the Mission; intending to present, in one view, such memorials of his life and death as we have been able to collect.

Launcelot Byrd Minor was the son of Gen. John Minor, of Hazle Hill, near Fredericksburg, Va., and Lucy Landon, daughter of Landon Carter, Esq., of King George county, Va.; and was born on the 9th of September, 1813, at "Topping Castle," Caroline county, the country seat of his parents. We may trace to a very early period in his life, those strongly marked traits of character, which, when sanctified by Divine grace, peculiarly fitted him for the work of a *pioneer* in the service of the Church. His philanthropy was ardent and expansive, his benevolence disinterested and self-sacrificing; and to these moral qualities, he added a natural love of enterprize and adventure, a courage insensible to danger, and great powers of physical endurance. Narratives of travel were the favorite books of his boyhood, and among them, he was especially delighted with the story of Mungo Park. Even in early childhood, he seems to have manifested an interest in Africa and her degraded children. With an older brother and sister, he was accustomed to deposit a portion of his little savings in a joint money box, whose contents were carefully hoarded to aid the benevolent designs of the Colonization Society. His diligence in reading Rollin's Ancient History was rewarded, by his mother, with the sum of twenty-five cents a volume; and this, augmented by the profits of his own industry in the manufacture of little boxes and other similar articles, was brought to his sister "for the Missionaries in Africa."

When quite young, Launcelot was entrusted to the care of an uncle in Louisa county, where he remained several years. This relative is described as "a wise man in the education of his children; a true patriot of the old stamp, full of ideas of Roman simplicity and virtue; designing to bring up his children in habits of hardihood and virtuous exertion of mind and body." It is easy to discern the effects of this early training, in the future character of the pupil. His love of rambling and athletic sports was, at times, rather too apparent in his soiled and tattered garments. On one occasion, his mother remonstrated with him on the reckless wear and

tear to which his apparel was subjected. His reply was
characteristic; "Mother, I want to make them hardy."
He was reminded that his heedlessness was sinful, as
the money, thus expended, might be more usefully employed. The admonition was not lost; for the clothes
were always found, when not in use, carefully brushed
and laid away, with a cloth spread over them. The incident was worthy of note as evincing a strong regard
to principle in one so young. His subsequent school-boy
days were spent at Edgewood, Hanover county, and
when about sixteen years of age, he became a student at
Kenyon College. At the close of the year, having lent
the money which had been provided for his expenses,
he set off for home on foot; and twice afterwards accomplished the whole journey, a distance of four hundred miles, in the same way. The exposure to which
he was subjected on these occasions, was, however, a
permanent injury to his health. It was the cause of a
rheumatic affection which never ceased to trouble him,
and which so contracted the sinew of his right thumb,
that writing became an irksome and painful exercise.
It was in one of these journeys just referred to, that an
incident occurred, strongly illustrative of some points in
his character. He was in Canada, on his way to New-
York, when he met with a poor Irish boy in distress,
having no one to direct or assist him. Launcelot had
in his possession, besides a draft which he thought
could not be cashed until he reached New-York, scarcely
money enough to defray his own expenses; but this was
not to be considered an obstacle to his benevolence.
With characteristic disinterestedness, he became the

lad's patron, and undertook, by some means or other, to convey him to his friends. Of course, this could not be accomplished without much self-denying exertion. Whenever it was possible, they proceeded on foot, and when this could not be done, they travelled in the cheapest manner. At one time, Minor himself, ate nothing for twenty-four hours, lest his little stock should be exhausted before they reached the end of their journey. Having taken a deck passage on one of the boats for himself and the boy, he overheard the cabin passengers disputing about some point, upon which his excellent memory furnished the desired information. Forgetting the position in which he had chosen to place himself, he joined in the discussion. This called forth some rude expression of contempt for the opinion of a deck passenger, which Launcelot's somewhat fiery spirit could not brook, and a rather serious altercation ensued. Meanwhile, a party of the lad's countrymen, having learned something of the kindness of his young friend, could hardly be restrained from deciding the argument with the shelalah.

Mr. Minor seems to have been, naturally, of a diffident and reserved disposition. One of his relations writes: " His diffidence, indeed almost feminine bashfulness, was, I remember, great. I do not think he talked much, but if roused, his earnestness was beautiful. The diffidence of which I speak, would not have extended to such a degree as to prevent him from expressing himself decidedly, if need were, on any subject, for there was an independence and recklessness of danger in his character, which would have graced an ancient martyr. On one occasion, (I cannot remember the subject of conversation, for I was quite a child, but the circumstance made a deep impression on my mind,) I was at his sister's, there were several persons present, and he took little part in what was passing, looked embarrassed, and, I believed, almost suffered from their presence. Gradually, the conversation grew animated, and some individual took, what he considered, a false position. Principle was involved—he became instantly roused; forgetful of all previous timidity, he rose from his leaning position, sat erect, his eye brightened, his countenance changed, and he waited for an opportunity to speak. A pause at last ensued; gently, but with firmness, a decision and earnestness, you could scarcely have expected from one so shrinking, he pointed out errors involved in the opinion, showed the evil consequences which would result from it, then, with simplicity and clearness, "speaking the truth in love," directed the mind to what he believed was right, as "founded upon true principles."

CHAPTER XV.

MR. MINOR was blessed with a devotedly pious mother, whose efforts to interest his youthful mind in the concerns of eternity, seem not to have been in vain. She had sown carefully the seeds of Divine truth and watered them with her prayers, and she watched, with anxious solicitude, for the fruits of her labor. But though, for a time, her faith was tried by apparent delay, the work was going on, unseen. The buried germ was preparing to send forth the vigorous shoot. He seems to have been the subject of early religious convictions, although his natural reserve prevented him from communicating his feelings.

While in college, he was attacked by dangerous illness, and now his mother's solicitude for his eternal interests became almost overpowering. While her own fervent supplications were ascending in behalf of her sick child, she implored her Christian friends to unite with her in interceding for his conversion. She also sent a similar request to the clergymen of almost every denomination in Fredericksburg, and there seems to have been a remarkable coincidence between these especial prayers and the change which now took place in his character. Hitherto, he had been ever correct in his moral deportment, and exhibited, in all his conduct in reference to religious things, the general influence of his mother's faithful instructions ; but his heart remained yet untouched by the constraining love of Christ. He had not so realized his lost condition by nature, as to know the full value of the price paid for his redemption. He had not yet learned to cling to the cross of Christ as his only refuge from the wrath to come, and to recognize, in that exhibition of divine love, the all-powerful motive for entire consecration to the service of his Redeemer. But now, when there seemed but a step between him and death, the light of eternity revealed the true importance of the lessons which had been familiar to him, even from infancy, and, with full purpose of heart, he resolved that henceforth he would live, not unto himself, but unto Him who had died for him. Henceforward, with his natural fearlessness and firmness of character, directed and confirmed by the Spirit of God, he pressed forward with unfaltering step in the race upon which he had entered. He had enlisted, with entire determination, under the banner of his Redeemer, and manfully did he continue the conflict unto his life's end. No prospect of toil, of suffering or of death, could deter him from any field where a triumph was to be won in the cause of his Divine Master. His was just such a spirit as we should naturally select to stand in the post of danger ; and we do not wonder that, when he had resolved to enter the ministry, he should be led to exercise his office in the very midst of the hostile hosts.

In the early part of his college course, he had seen, in an old almanac, the statement that six hundred millions of his fellow men still remained in heathen darkness ; and, from that time, as he afterwards told a clerical friend, his mind was made up, that if he should ever become a Christian, he would be also a missionary.

His determination to devote himself to the work of the ministry, was formed immediately after the change recorded above. He entered the Theological Seminary near Alexandria, D. C., in the autumn of 1833, and during his course of study, was actively engaged in seeking the temporal and spiritual good of the destitute in that neighborhood. He was the founder of a Sunday school at Falls Church which he attended with untiring zeal, and though obliged to walk seven miles to reach it, was never absent, however severe might be the weather.

In the course of his journies through the United States and Canada, he had become much interested in the poor aborigines of our own forest, and, at one time, thought of devoting himself to a mission among them. Being dissuaded from this, by his friends, he turned his attention to China, which then appeared to be the only foreign field open to missionaries of our Church. While, with the enlarged view of a Christian philanthropist, he acknowledged the whole world as the field of missionary enterprise, he was earnestly inquiring in what portion of that field, God would have him labor. At the Virginia Convention, in 1834, the Rev. Dr. Milnor, then Secretary and General Agent of the Foreign Committee, announced the desire of that body to attempt, once
6*

more, the establishment of a mission in West Africa, and
exhorted the students of the seminary prayerfully to
consider the question of duty in reference to that unhappy country. About this time, a prayer-circle was
formed among those whose attention had been turned towards the foreign field, in which Boone, Savage, Payne
and Minor were accustomed to unite their supplications
for Divine guidance. Who can doubt that they obtained
the blessing thus fervently sought? The following letter
will show the state of Minor's feelings at that time. It
was addressed to his mother, and bears the date

"June 27th, 1836

" From all that I can learn, there is no longer any
doubt but that white men must go to Africa. And
now, dear mother, comes the question, ' is it my duty to
go ?' I feel entirely unable to decide the question, and
therefore shall endeavor to leave all things in the hands
of God. God willing, I propose setting apart next Saturday, as a day of fasting and prayer for Divine assistance. I wish you and all the family to pray with me.
Let me hear from you, if possible, before then. Farewell, dearest mother ! that God may strengthen and
support you in the hour of trial shall be the constant
prayer of your son,

" L. B. MINOR."

The request contained in this letter, was faithfully
observed by his excellent mother, and the result was
most remarkable. Hitherto, her feelings had been
strongly opposed to her son going any where abroad,

especially to Africa. The day passed, and with it passed, at once and forever, the last lingering desire to oppose the holy calling of her child—the last struggle of reluctant nature to set up its claims in opposition to the supreme authority of the Redeemer's last command. The effect of that day's solemn exercises upon Minor's own mind, is communicated in his next letter.

"THEOLOGICAL SEMINARY, *July* 6, 1836.

"DEAR MOTHER :—I was much disappointed at not receiving an answer to my last letter. But the day is now passed, and you are waiting to hear the result. After a calm and prayerful consideration of the subject, it is my firm conviction that Africa is the field of labor allotted me by God. To Africa, I am willing, nay, anxious, to go. I thank my heavenly Father, that the trial has not been greater than I could bear. His grace alone has supported me, and I feel assured, my dear mother, that you also will be assisted by the same Spirit. Many of my fears with regard to the climate have been removed."

The important question was now finally decided. We have noticed his early interest in the poor degraded race to whom he now devoted his life, and we know that interest had been unabated through his college course, when he still continued his contribution to the Colonization Society, from the proceeds of a small patch of ground cultivated for the purpose. How far these circumstances affected his decision, we cannot, perhaps, determine; but we are assured that he was greatly in-

fluenced by the consideration of that heavy debt, due to
the oppressed people, from American Christians.

In the summer of 1836, soon after his ordination, he
received his appointment from the Foreign Committee,
and was for some months employed, in conjunction with
his colleague, Rev. John Payne, in presenting the claims
of their cause in Maryland and Virginia. Of his efforts
at this time, we have, from his own pen, only the following little record.

"RICHMOND, *January* 4, 1837.

"My reception has uniformly been hospitable. Discouragements have been mingled with comforts. One
person said within my hearing, that he had no intention
of going to Africa. For bitterness of soul I could have
wept. A poor widow came to the roadside to put in
my hand twenty-five cents. She said it was all she had,
but her prayers should go with it, and as she spoke,
tears ran down her care- worn countenance. I said
within myself, surely God, who hath opened the heart
of this widow, will never permit his servants to want."

Bishop Meade, who was with him on this occasion,
remembers that the young missionary mingled his tears
with those of the humble Christian, who thus evinced
her sympathy in the work to which his heart was given.
Several months were thus spent in passing from parish
to parish, and preaching as he had opportunity. His
success in awakening interest and in collecting funds, is
mentioned in the "Spirit of Missions" for this date, as
affording "encouraging evidence that the cause of Africa

is coming near to many hearts, that the Church will be sustained, and her missionaries encouraged in the Mission."

In one of the few fragments of journal found among his papers, he mentions having preached at Fredericksburg, the home of his family, with some little discomfort, and expresses some apprehensions as to the depressing effect of the African climate; but concludes with—"God is my helper, therefore I will not fear. Without his assistance, I am nothing. Man is but vapor." On the opposite side was irregularly written:— 'Never shall it be said that the sable chieftain from the African coast sought, in vain, for the Gospel. Farewell-dearest mother! Farewell, dearest mother!"

The sermon concerning Africa, of which he probably made frequent use at the time, is preserved. It commences with a congratulation on the position which the Church had assumed in the General Convention of 1835; dwells on the debt due to Africa, both from England and America; exhibits, undisguisedly, the difficulties of the Mission on which he had been appointed, yet speaks confidently of its success; refers to the continuance of the slave trade, and urges missionary enterprize as its most effectual check; and throughout, shows the deepest sense of the entire dependence of all such labors upon the help and blessing of the Lord. The commencement of his plans and purposes, simple as they were, corresponds so entirely with what he actually attempted and accomplished, that it deserves a record here. Thus he wrote: "By God's help, we will not suffer them to call in vain. We will take of these children, so freely offered us, as many as we can attend to, and educate them thoroughly. They will become boarders in our houses, nor will we suffer them to hold any intercourse with their parents, unless in our presence, lest they become corrupted by evil example. As many as God, by his grace, shall see fit to convert, we will have ordained and sent forth as missionaries of the cross to their benighted countrymen. Those who are not called, but who have received a good education, we will employ as teachers of schools throughout the land." Faithfully did he persevere in the course which he here marked out, and if the high hopes with which he looked forward to the result, have not all been realized, it is because there have been so few to carry on the work which he was so soon summoned to relinquish. Who can tell what glorious harvests might have been reaped, had laborers, like-minded with himself, been furnished in numbers at all proportionate to the extent and promise of the field !

Mr. Minor's preaching was such as might have been expected from the view we have already taken of his character. He was a man eminently in earnest in what he undertook. "He preached," says a brother in the ministry, who, like him, has chosen his sphere of duty in a foreign field,* "as he thought and felt, seriously, decidedly, pointedly, energetically." "The course of one of Mr. Minor's sermons is often like one of St. Paul's epistles; there is a real, substantial, and close succession of argument, but there is none of the mere apparatus of arrangement. Of dialectic argument, however, he exhibits few traces. He usually employed the shorter and

* Rev. Mr. Syle, Missionary to China.

more direct method of appealing, at once, to the con-
sciences of his hearers, and exhibited an impatience of
anything which approached to trifling in religious matters." We proceed to give a few extracts from his discourses, which will show how much of his material was
drawn from his own deep feelings and convictions, according to the Apostolic principles. "We speak that
we do know and testify that we have seen." In a sermon on Heb. xi. i, we find this definition of faith: "perfect trust or confidence in God ; such confidence as
would make you willing, yea, anxious to cast all things
into his hands; such trust as would induce you to follow his directions, though they seem to lead to instant
destruction."

On Luke xviii. 1, speaking of the infidel's objections
to prayer, he remarks that such objections "proceed not,
as they would have us believe, from superior intelligence
and free thinking, but from ignorance and from not thinking at all on the subject." Again, on a similar topic :
"Verily the evidence of divine revelation is abundantly
bright and overwhelming. The difficulty lies, not in
the lack of evidence, but in the depraved heart of the ob-
jector. Man would soon come to doubt that two and
two make four, did it put the same restraint on his evil
passions, as is placed there by the religion of Christ."
Of such as are not yet convinced of their entire inability
to do any good thing "as of themselves," he says :
"Their desire is to act the part of a master workman,
while the spirit performs the part of a humble assistant."
One more extract will suffice ; the happiness of reunion
after death is his theme. "Who will describe the joy

of the Christian mother, who finds that of the little flock
committed to her care, not one is wanting, but each one
is there, to sing the praises of the Redeemer, who bought
them with his blood!   How will the missionary of the
cross, whose bones whitened in distant lands, rejoice to
embrace his long lost friends and relations.

CHAPTER XVI.

On the eighteenth of May, 1837, Mr. Minor sailed from Baltimore, in company with the Rev. Mr. Payne and his wife, for Cape Palmas. His feelings on taking leave of his native land are expressed in the following letter:

> " Brig Baltimore, *Chesapeake Bay*,
>   May 19th, 1837.

Dear Mother—I continued to look after the boat that bore you from me, hoping to catch one more glimpse of my dear mother, and succeeded in distinguishing your bonnet. I felt that I had parted with a friend, in comparison with whom, all others were cold and heartless. Your boat proceeded rapidly towards Baltimore, while we remained almost motionless. After beating against a head wind for some hours, with little success, we came to anchor, and remained there until daybreak. The next morning, taking advantage of an ebb tide, the anchor was weighed, and we floated down the bay without the slightest assistance from the wind, until about noon, when a light breeze filled the sails and slightly increased our motion. Nothing of consequence has

occurred.   The sick are doing well, and would do
better if they could be induced to obey orders.   This
however is not to be expected.   The wind has increased
somewhat since I commenced writing.   This period of
calm, or rather of gentle motion, I have embraced to
write to my dear mother, fearing that sickness might
prevent me, when opportunity offers.   Our captain is
very kind and attentive, and we are comfortable.   I
could be happy were it not for the fear that my mother
is suffering on my account.

"May be, if your prayers were of a general nature
occasionally, you would enjoy more comfort.   Pray for
the heathen, not for those alone among whom your son
has gone to labor, but for all.   Pray, not only for your
children, but for the children of all your neighbors and
friends.   In watering others, you, yourself, will be
watered.   Dear mother, farewell.

"L. B. MINOR."

The voyage afforded no incident of sufficient importance to claim a notice here, but the following may be of
some interest.

June 13*th*, 1837.

"Dear mother—The 'trade winds' are here, but not
as we expected.   Instead of a regular, steady breeze,
we have had head winds, light winds, and no winds at
all.   Our progress of course was slow, but we are here
at last, thank God !   Porto Praya, St. Jago, June 13th.
'June 14th—I have been ashore.   Such a town,
such a country, and such a people, never did my eyes

behold! Almost the first object I met, was a huge negro covered with leprosy from head to foot. Had I the power, I would not describe him; it was too horrible. He is literally a being without hope in this world or in the world to come. Oh! that God would have mercy on his soul! The bare thought of, him almost brings tears into my eyes.

"June 15th. * * * * * * * * * We shall probably go to sea this evening. Farewell, dearest mother! My love to all; pray for me.

"L. B. MINOR."

He arrived at his future home on the 4th of July, and on the following day, we find him writing to his affectionate mother as follows:

C. P. MISSION HOUSE,
West Africa, July 5th, 1837.

"MY DEAR MOTHER—I am in Africa—yet live. I have breathed the tainted atmosphere, yet have no fear. We arrived at this place yesterday in good health, twenty-seven days after leaving Baltimore. Our passage from the Cape de Verdes was long and tedious, but I do not regret it. It gave me an opportunity of examining my heart, whether it was prepared for eternity, should God see fit to call me from the world. Sometimes, the thought would arise in my mind that I was rushing, uncalled, into the presence of my Maker; but generally, the grace of God was with me. Indeed, I enjoyed religion during the voyage as much, if not more, than at any previous period. My sufferings from seasickness were by no means light, or of short duration.

"We were under serious apprehensions lest we should find no one left to greet us, but to our inexpressible joy Dr. Savage met us on the beach. Regardless of appearances, we leaped on shore and embraced him, much to the amusement of the natives.

"After dining with Mr. Wilson, Dr. Savage and myself went to the Mission house. The situation is high, I should think a hundred feet above the level of the sea. So far, it has proved healthy. The view is most beautiful, and the scenery rich beyond description.

"Judging from the appearance of the natives, this country is healthy. I never saw a more athletic set of men. At all events, we will give the climate a fair trial. If then we fall, it is in our Master's cause.

* * * * * * * * * * * * * * * * * * *

"My communications hereafter will be as frequent as my health will permit. Dr. S. is opposed to my writing much. For some time we shall avoid all labor, both physical and mental. If God gives us health, we hope to use it for his glory. Farewell, dear mother; give my love to all the family and pray for your son.

"L. B. MINOR."

We make a short extract from a letter addressed to the Foreign Secretary, a few days later.

"We have at length reached the scene of action, and are calmly waiting for the fever. God, in his mercy, has removed from our minds all dread whatsoever. Indeed, we can scarcely realize that air so bland and soft as this, can be so deleterious to human life. But it is even so. Possibly I am, at this moment, writing the last line I shall ever direct to you, and if so, dear brother, farewell until we meet where pain and sickness come no more."

It will appear from the above extracts, that Mr. Minor was fully aware of the danger to be encountered from the unfriendly climate of Africa. To the objections of his friends, his reply was decided and conclusive. "If every foot print were on the grave of a missionary, still the command must be obeyed: 'Go ye into all the world and preach the Gospel to every creature.' A relative said to him, 'you will not live ten years in Africa.' 'True,' he replied, 'true, my dear cousin, but may I not do more in ten years, for the kingdom of Christ in Africa,· than I could in seventy here? Let me crowd the actions of a century in ten years—'twere sweeter than to rust out a life time.'"

In the acclimating fever Mr. Minor was dangerously ill, but God preserved his life, and we find his next letter dated

"CAPE PALMAS, *December* 25, 1837.

"Contrary to the opinion of many, I am spared once more to address you. The dreaded ordeal has been passed, yet we not only live, but are enabled to do some little in the vineyard of our Master, while a bright prospect of usefulness is opening before us. That we have suffered, cannot be denied, but that suffering has by no means exceeded our expectation. This unfortunate, degraded land, has been clothed with terrors not its own. Hundreds, whites, are now residing on this coast in the enjoyment of good health. They who have hitherto cloaked their coldness under this plea, must now seek some more plausible excuse. There is risk to be run; there is suffering to be endured, but surely the follower of Christ can never consider this a sufficient reason why he should remain idle, while the plentiful harvest lies before him, not only fit for the sickle, but falling, wasting, perishing, for lack of laborers. Far be it from me to urge my brethren to rush headlong to the work, without thought or sufficient preparation; nor, on the other hand, would I have them tarry, in the vain expectation that God, by some unusual method, shall bid them go forward to their work. We do not urge them to come to our assistance; our great desire is, not that this station flourish, but that the wants of the heathen generally, should have its due weight in the minds of Christians, though the fault will be ours, if minute and accurate information be wanting with regard to the people among whom we labor. It would be difficult to conceive of a people more degraded, more utterly dead to every moral sense, than those who daily surround us. In vain have we sought for one good quality, one bright spot to enliven the dark picture. We are informed that a short time previous to our arrival, five persons were tried by 'sassa wood,' only two of whom escaped with their lives. Among the number of those who perished, was a man far advanced in life, whose only offence, if report be true, was the possession of a rice farm, which, by rather more than ordinary industry, he had rendered somewhat superior to those of his neighbors. He swallowed the poisonous liquid, but seemed likely to recover.

This, however, was by no means agreeable to the wishes or intentions of his judges; so, seizing him by the feet, they dragged him down a steep, rocky hill, where, continuing to dash him violently against the ground, they speedily succeeded in extinguishing the vital spark. His fertile field was the reward of their iniquity. The word of a priest or doctor is alone sufficient to subject a person to this terrible ordeal.

"Such are the people among whom we live and labor. Though not entirely without hope of benefitting the adult, our eyes are much directed to the younger portion of the community. The number contained in the male school is at present small; they are, however, without exception, promising boys. Did my health permit, I could speedily increase their number, and hope to do so within the next month. Feeble health must necessarily prove a great drawback to our operations, and though the field of labor before us is highly encouraging, little fruit can be expected within the next three or four years."

From the the close of this letter, it will be seen that he had commenced his duties by taking charge of the school at Mt. Vaughan. His next communication contains more definite information with regard to his pupils.

"CAPE PALMAS, *January* 14, 1838.

" In vain would I attempt to convey to you an adequate idea of the pleasure afforded us by the letters per brig Niobe. Surely if our friends could but realize our feelings, their communications would be more frequent.

But none, save those who, like ourselves, have for months been separated, not only from friends, but from the world generally, can ever understand our emotions on an occasion, such as the one just mentioned. Still less can they sympathise with the bitter disappointment caused by an arrival which brings nothing for us; no, not even a newspaper.

" Though we cannot entertain the hope that a saving change has, in any instance, actually taken place, still we are cheered by the belief that our efforts have not been entirely useless. In morals, a very decided improvement is manifest among the scholars. Only a few months since, we were almost daily called upon to lament their want of probity and veracity. But now, thanks to Almighty God! the case is far different. It is seldom that we have cause even to doubt their word ; and if theft has been committed during the past two months, we know it not. We do not pretend to say that they are faultless; far from it. Faults are committed, and that frequently ; but lying and stealing are not among them. This is the more remarkable, as the natives are peculiarly prone to those sins, which with them are reckoned no disgrace.

" My room has become quite a resort for them. It is true, that such of my books as contain pictures are somewhat the worse for their visits; still I encourage them, as it enables me to draw them into familiar conversation, and thereby, to obtain a more intimate knowledge of their respective characters. The interest manifested in religion, is decidedly greater than is usual among boys of the same age in America. They also profess an ardent desire for a new heart, and solemnly declare that, never more, will they have anything to do with devil-men or gree-grees, but that the God of heaven shall be their God. The regularity with which they attend their devotions would shame many professing Christians. Their views, as might be expected, are imperfect and confused.

" A portion of the day is regularly devoted by the boys, to labor, and we entertain the hope that they will, in a short time, contribute somewhat to their own support. In order to attach them more firmly to the Mission, we have given to each a small spot of ground, to cultivate as they may think proper. There are now growing on the Mission premises, bananas, plantains, lemons, oranges, limes, sour-sop, sweet-sop, arrowroot, cassada, pine-apples, potatoes, corn, yams, coffee and guavas, besides various kinds of American vegetables. Could you send us a few bread-fruit plants from the West Indies, it would materially improve our stock ; a few of these trees would furnish a large amount of wholesome food.

" As you may suppose, my duties are various, and to some degree, onerous ; but when I look around on the docile little flock who tell me, ' I be fader for dem now,' I feel that the wealth of the world could not afford greater pleasure than my present duties."

Even at this early period of his residence in Africa, it is remarked of Mr. Minor by his associates, that he " has made good progress in the language of the Grebo, and he seems to possess an unusual tact at acquiring

7

their phrases and converting them to a practical purpose."

In August and September, 1838, he made the two visits to Garraway, which have been already mentioned in the former part of this work. We find the following notice of the failure of his attempt to establish a station there, among the very few and brief records of his journal.

"*Sept.* 13, 1838.

"Yesterday I returned from Garraway. They appeared to care little whether I came among them or not, and some were actually opposed to it. Why this change of sentiment ? On my first visit it was not so. Duke treated me as well as he knew how, but I suffered much from mortification. No one spake comfortably to me. Those to whom I had a right to look for consolation, seemed rather to delight in adding to my sufferings. It seemed so to me. God forgive me if I do them wrong. But I humbly trust that my afflictions have been, and will be, sanctified to me. The mortifications that I suffered on the occasion showed me, what I ought to have known before, that pride had made for itself a dwelling place in my heart."

CHAPTER XVII.

EARLY in April, 1839, Mr. Minor availed himself of an opportunity of visiting the Gold Coast, with a view to acquire such information as might determine the question of its eligibility as a field for future effort. He arrived in the United States in July, and communicated the result of his observations, to the Board of Missions, in the following document:

"FREDERICKSBURG, VA., *Sept.* 20, 1839.

"Circumstances over which I could exercise no control, have prevented me from sooner complying with your request to render some account of my late visit to that part of Africa called the Gold Coast; and even now, I must confine myself to the subject of Missions. Though a resident for nearly two years on the coast of Africa, the state of things at the Gold Coast did not cease to excite my surprise. Instead of savages in the lowest barbarism, as in other parts of Africa, the natives had here made considerable advances in civilization; indeed, some of the more wealthy had been well educated, and lived in a style of comfort and even splendor.

Their spacious mansions and well spread boards were
open to all ; and the way-faring man and the stranger
were especially welcome. They were surrounded by
numerous slaves and retainers, ready, in case of need,
to defend their houses, which, in many instances, are so
constructed as to answer well the purpose of fortifications. Indeed, of one house, I saw the ramparts mount-
ed with a battery of cannon. Nor are these precautions
taken without sufficient grounds ; for the day has not long
gone by, when the Ashantees, the scourge of that portion
of the continent, threatened the utter annihilation of
their settlements.

" For nearly three centuries, the greatest portion of
the Gold Coast has been in the hands of Europeans, who,
for the security of their trade, have built forts and cas-
tles of a strength and size almost incredible to those who
have not seen them; nor is it easy to conceive how such
stupendous structures could have been erected on a coast
so remote and so barbarous.

" Although the early records of these establishments
are now lost, or locked up in the archives of some European government, yet there can be but little doubt that
they owe their origin to the slave trade, when that traf-
fic was legal. No legal trade now carried on, would
justify such expense ; nor does it require such extensive
fortifications for its protection ; most of them being deserted, their tottering ramparts now serve no other purpose than to add to the picturesque features of the coast.
One, among them, bears the name of my native town,
Fredericksburg. Many, however, are still garrisoned
and in good order ; and populous villages have grown up

around them. The Dutch castle of ' Elmira' is said to mount a hundred pieces of cannon, some of which are of enormous size, and, viewed from the sea, its frowning battlements and lofty towers present an imposing appearance. But though this portion of the coast is fraught with interest, to the missionary it is especially so. Many of the natives here, as I before remarked, have been well educated in Europe, and many more have been taught to read in the schools kept at some of the forts. The former invariably profess the Christian faith, though but too often disregarding its precepts. The latter, anterior to the arrival of the Wesleyan missionaries, had scarcely any ideas on the subject of religion. It has seldom happened that the heralds of salvation have entered on a field more promising, or have had the path more fully laid open to them, than was the case of those who first visited this coast. In the public schools before mentioned, the Bible is the text book, and though little pains have been bestowed to instruct the pupils in its meaning, they comprehend and retain many of its precepts, which, through the blessing of God, will, with time and culture, greatly fructify in this long neglected soil. Several young men, convinced by what they read, that they had a soul to be saved or lost, and being unable to gain any information from the nominal Christians around them, were in the habit of retiring to a solitary spot, on the shores of a small lake, there to read and meditate upon the wonderful things contained in that book. Their feelings, as the plan of salvation gradually unfolded itself to their view, can only be understood by those who have experienced similar sensa-

tions. But though shut out from the Christian world,
and surrounded by those who knew not, and cared not
for the name of Jesus, their Heavenly Father was not
unmindful of his little flock in the wilderness. Just
when most needed, a missionary, bearing the glad tidings
of salvation, made his appearance among them.

"No sooner was his purpose known, than he was surrounded by anxious inquirers, eager to receive the words
of life as they fell from his lips. He had not, as is usual
with missionaries, to endure severe trials of faith, or to
wait long for the first fruits of his labors. Numbers
pressed forward as candidates for baptism, and since then
six or seven hundred have been received. But as intellectual belief is all that is required by the missionaries
previous to administering that ordinance, it is impossible
to speak with certainty as to the amount of good done,
though, without doubt, it is considerable.

"At this time there are on the gold coast, but two
European missionaries. One, a Dane, lives forty or fifty
miles inland from the British Accra, believing that he
enjoys better health there than on the coast; the other
(Mr. Freeman) an English Wesleyan Methodist, who resides at Cape Coast Castle. From him I learned that the
Wesleyans had, by means of native assistants, occupied
most of the important villages between Cape Coast and
British Accra, and expected to extend their operations as
far as Coomasse, the capital of the Ashantee empire,
whence he then had very lately returned. His reception
by its bloodthirsty and despotic prince, was decidedly favorable, despite of an active opposition on the part of
some Mohammedan moolahs, who were anxious to in-

troduce the doctrines of their own faith. During his stay
in the metropolis, twenty-five or thirty human victims
were sacrificed, to attend in the next world on the king's
brother, who died of fatigue, encountered during an exhibition gotten up in honor of the arrival of a European.
The Wesleyans do not propose to extend their operations
further eastward than Cape Coast. Thus will Elmira
and the Fort villages eastward of it be left destitute unless
occupied, as Mr. Freeman is desirous they should be, by
American missionaries. They do not, however, present
the same advantages for missionary labor as the country
lying on the east side of Cape Coast; for there are no
schools save at Elmira, and there Dutch is only taught,
which would avail little towards smoothing the way of
an American.

"But with these drawbacks, the Fort villages present
some points of advantage, only to be found where the
European authority is acknowledged. Among these,
may be reckoned the disposition, now almost universal
among the natives, to adopt the form, at least, of Christianity, and to procure for their children, the advantages
of a good education. We may add to these facilities the
entire security of the missionary and his family from
lawless violence, and the ease with which subsistence
may be procured. A missionary at Elmira might rent
a comfortable house at a reasonable rate, and having
brought with him a moderate supply of necessaries,
might, before fever came on, surround himself with
most of the comforts and conveniences of life. At the
Forts, still further westward, he would find fewer conveniences. Elmira is, by far, the most populous of the

settlements on the gold coast, unless we consider the
three Accras as one, but it is not accounted the most
healthful; nor is it certain how far the Dutch authorities
would regard the efforts of the Americans.   Mr. Free
man recommended Dix Cove as a point well suited fo.
the commencement of operations.   Though for almost
two centuries the acknowledged subjects of the British
crown, the inhabitants still retain many of their wild and
barbarous customs, and, at this day, render homage to
a crocodile, the tenant of a pond near the village, making
him frequent offerings of white fowls.   So completely
tame has the animal become, that upon the cry of the
fowl he comes fearlessly out to receive the fluttering
victims at the hands of the devotee, and then quietly
returns to his watery home.

"There are, at Dix Cove, several young men professing Christianity, having received instruction and
baptism at Cape Coast.   When they heard that I was
a missionary, they came forward to greet me, as one of
whose friendship and kindness there could be no doubt.
During the stay, we held a meeting and had much conversation, but the medium through which we communicated with each other was so imperfect that it was
impossible to determine, with certainty, the degree of
their religious attainments.   For docility of disposition,
however, few can surpass them.   A devoted and active
missionary might easily engage the more intelligent of
these as teachers, and as many more as needed might
be procured at Cape Coast, who are fully capable, under strict supervision, of giving instruction in the rudiments of education."

CHAPTER XVIII.

Mr. Minor's visit to the United States—His marriage and return to Africa—Efforts in the Colony—Letters.

MR. MINOR's visit to the United States was stated in the "Spirit of Missions," to be "in accordance with the advice of his brethren, for the benefit of his health, for obtaining priests' orders, and for other purposes connected with the interests of the mission."

We find no record of the time which he spent in this country, but cannot doubt that it was actively and usefully employed. Some of it was passed in visiting his family and friends, who would gladly have detained him among them, but he was impatient to return to his work. To one who urged his longer stay, he writes thus:

"BALTIMORE, *January* 22d, 1840.

"MY DEAR BROTHER:—Yours of January 16th reached me last night. I feel most sincerely grateful for the interest you manifest in my welfare, but hope you will not think me wilful, when I say, I cannot tarry; it is the cause of my soul. In Africa is the portion of my Master's vineyard which he has committed to my care. It is wasted and desolate, for there is no man to till it. How can I be content to tarry, lest God should say to me, as he said to his prophet of old, 'What

7*

doest thou here, Elijah?' I was called to preach the Gospel in Africa, not to act as travelling agent in America. * * * * * * * * * *

" Farewell, your brother,

" L. B. MINOR."

One of his kind relatives, anxious to secure for him such comforts as might contribute to the preservation of his health, offered him some important assistance, provided he would reserve it for his own personal benefit, and not "squander" it upon the children of his charge. He promised to consider the offer, and soon returned answer that he would rather not receive anything, on such conditions.

On the 23rd of January, 1840, Mr. Minor was married to Miss Mary Stewart, of Baltimore, a communicant of St. Peter's Church in that city. On the 15th of February he sailed with his wife and the Rev. Joshua Smith, from Norfolk, and arrived at Cape Palmas on the fifth of April.

During his absence, a small chapel had been erected near the Mission house at Mt. Vaughan, chiefly for the benefit of the neighboring colonists ; and of this little church, Mr. Minor now consented to become the Pastor. He assumed this charge from a sense of duty, although he had always felt a decided preference for a station more entirely among the natives ; and he would frequently say : " In order to their good, I must throw myself among them ; I must become as one of them ; they must feel, as they would say, that I am their ' God man.' " As long, however as his brethren deemed it

expedient for him to remain at Mt. Vaughan, he devoted
all his energies to the spiritual good of the flock here
committed to his care. He was their kind and sympathising friend and adviser in all their temporal and
spiritual difficulties, and wherever want and suffering
required relief, his charities were generally scattered.

The following appears to be one of the earliest letters
which he wrote after his return from the United States.

"CAPE PALMAS, *May* 28*th*, 1840.

" For some weeks past we have had a minature
specimen of the deluge, and probably such a one as is
seldom seen, even in this region of the world. For more
than four weeks, the rain has fallen in torrents, almost
incessantly, keeping us close prisoners, and not unfre-
quently coming through the roof to visit us. Yet for all
that, we are alive and merry. Both Mr. Smith and my
wife have passed through the fever, the latter with as
little suffering, probably, as any white person that ever
visited Liberia. Either the climate has become more
salubrious, or the mode of treatment now pursued, is far
more judicious. At all events, the danger to be appre-
hended by new comers is many degrees less now, than
formerly.

" Our mission is in a highly prosperous condition,
and some of our pupils are prepared to become assistant
teachers. We are confidently looking forward to the day,
and that not very far distant, when they will be prepared
to go forth themselves as teachers, and raise up others
to go forth as they have done. We ourselves will continue to exercise strict supervision over the whole, that

all things may go on 'decently and in order.' Thus
you may readily perceive that in time, Deo Volente, the
whole country, within our reach, will, to a greater or
less degree, be brought under Christian influence."

A few months later, he writes thus :

" CAPE PALMAS, *September 24.*

" But crosses and inconveniences are to be classed
among those trials with which God, in his mercy and
love, sees fit to afflict us.   It would ill become us to
complain of trials when our comforts are every day becoming greater, and are, even now, much more numerous
than we deserve.   We have lately fallen on a plan of
operating upon the natives, which we humbly hope, by
the Divine blessing, will eventuate in good.   It is the
endeavoring to induce a few of the more hopeful among
them to settle near us, and thus form a small village
under our immediate control, and from which all greegrees and sassa-wood palavers are, by express stipula-
tion, to be excluded ; nor will any working on Sunday
be allowed.   All to whom this plan has been proposed,
have readily agreed to it.   They are, to use their own
language, 'tired of country fash,' which is not surprising,
when we reflect that both their lives and property are
completely at the mercy of a lawless and unprincipled
soldiery.   We propose limiting the number, at first, to
ten families, and if the plan works well, to increase it
gradually, as our experience may suggest.

" There cannot be a doubt but that this branch of the
Mission, the colonists, imperiously demands our atten-

tion ; nor can it be neglected without detriment in more ways than one ; yet believing myself called of God, to preach the Gospel to the heathen, nothing short of it can render me contented. The bulk of the congregation on Sunday morning, is from the Mission—the average attendance from the colony at that time not exceeding twenty ; but at night, when other places of worship are closed, our little chapel is pretty well filled by a very attentive audience. Our Sunday school and Bible classes are, we humbly hope, doing good."

CHAPTER XIX.

Excursion into the country.

UNDER the date of February, 1841, Mr. Minor gives an interesting account of an excursion into the country. " Long confinement to a single spot, and to a somewhat monotonous routine of duty, rendering some recreation necessary, I left Mt. Vaughan, accompanied by a single native man, Gumino, and a small native boy who took advantage of our protection to return to his country, and whom I pressed into my service to make him carry for me a change of raiment. So very slight were my preparations, that no one at Mt. Vaughan supposed that we could intend being absent more than a day or two. I literally followed the command of Christ to His disciples, when He sent them forth to preach, for my change of raiment did not include a coat, and we had nothing with us whatever to purchase food. This was proceeding on a new plan, and altogether an experiment, but the possession of anything valuable to the natives had, in previous tours, been the cause of so much trouble and vexation, that it was determined, on the present occasion, to proceed without anything to tempt the cupidity of the lawless tribes through whom we must pass, but to trust

entirely to their hospitality for food and shelter. In consequence of these novel arrangements, our preparations
were on so very limited a scale, that when we disap-
peared in the bush behind Mt. Vaughan, all expected to
see us in a day or two ; even the missionaries knew not
whither we should bend our steps.   Even in my own
mind, it was by no means clear where we would go, but
this much, however, was fully determined on ; to go,
unless forcibly stopped, farther to the north-west than
any white man had ever gone before me, and, if practicable, to reach the head waters of Cavalla River, and
return to the beach by water.   Our first day's journey
lay through a region of country which has been described
more than once ; first a level and somewhat swampy
plain, then fine rolling uplands, watered by many
streams running to the north-east.   Three hours walk
from Mt. Vaughan we left the Grebo territory, and entered a frontier village, belonging to a subdivision of the
Nyambo tribe, called the Crabbo.   These people are at
war with another subdivision of the same tribe.   Less
than twenty individuals have lost their lives ; yet blood-
less, comparatively, as has been this quarrel, it has lasted
more than two years, and obliges both sides to keep a
sharp look out, as not more than two or three miles in-
tervene between their frontier towns.   Lounging around
the gate of Serare, the first town which we reached, we
found several men armed with muskets and cutlasses.
They rose when we approached, and saluted us politely.
Among them, my attendant recognized the most renowned warrior in that region, having slain five men
during the war, with his own hand.   This town is, from

its situation, so exposed to the attacks of the enemy, that
not more than half the men are allowed to go to their
farms at once ; a very serious hindrance in some countries, but by no means so in Africa, as the ordinary work
of two days may easily be accomplished in one, if the
cultivator desire it. Soraka, the chief town of the Crabbo,
is about two hours walk from Serare, and contains, probably, three thousand inhabitants, being one of the largest
towns in all that region ; yet we stopped only long enough
to salute the king, and pressed forward two hours farther, to
Kaka, the capital of the Bolebo country. During our
walk, we met a boy bearing a jar of honey as a present
to me from my friend, Krah of Bolebo, who informed me
that his father was absent. This information annoyed
us exceedingly, as we had not only expected to have tar-
ried with him during our stay in his town, but to have
him as our guide to the very country where he was gone.
We did not, however, lack for hospitality. Jedda, king
of Bolebo, did all in his power to make us comfortable.
Early the next morning, we sallied forth to examine the
surrounding country. Kaka has nothing remarkable in
its situation. The country is undulating, of moderate
fertility, but abounding in fine streams, which, joining
others from the Crabbo territory, form a river of some
magnitude, which, after precipitating itself over rocks
some twenty feet high, enters the sea at Fishtown,
twelve miles from Cape Palmas. Its width, at the
mouth, is probably fifty yards. This town, though it
holds a kind of prominence over the others, does not contain more than a thousand souls. The Bolebo is probably the smallest of all the subdivision of the Nyambo.

" The day after my arrival, I walked forth to enjoy the fresh air and to visit a small town about half a mile distant, on the top of a conical hill. The situation was very airy and pleasant, affording an extensive view of the surrounding country. The village was very small, not containing more than twenty huts, but the head man entertained us hospitably, with the best that the country afforded. Hearing that Saro, the capital of the Plebo country, was not more than two hours distant, I expressed a wish to visit it, which did not, however, meet with the approbation of the king and head-man of the town, who feared lest the honor of a visit from a white man should be divided with their neighbors ; but finding me bent upon it, they at length gave me a guide. Our road, which was little else than a foot path, led toward the north-east, over a large creek, which we crossed with difficulty, and, in about an hour, reached two small villages, situated on opposite hills not more than three hundred yards apart, one belonging to the Bolebo, the other to the Plebo ; a rather awkward situation for both, in case of war between those tribes. The country became more and more healthy as we proceeded, until we reached Saro. Wa, the king, a portly old man, did not, at first, receive us very cordially, complaining that although he was a man of distinction, I had brought him nothing. He was, however, graciously pleased to accept our excuse, that every town would have wished to stop us, had we any thing valuable in our possession, and we should never have seen his face. He kindly offered to prepare food for us, which being declined, he insisted on our accepting a goat as a present. This we could not refuse, but left it in his hands, to be brought to Mt. Vaughan at some future time.

"The threatening aspect of the clouds induced us to return to Ka, before we had time to admire, sufficiently, the romantically beautiful situation of Saro. In the evening I communicated to Ledda my wish to visit the Krebbo country. Though he had been aware of my wishes on the subject for several weeks, he now thought proper to express great astonishment, and endeavored to deter me, by setting forth the dangers of the way, and the ferocious character of the people. I was too well versed in African diplomacy, to put any manner of faith in the representations of my friend Tedda, though we knew that the Krebbo were reputed cannibals. Finding that we were not to be dissuaded, he at length consented to give us guides, which was all we wanted. After dark, I preached to the men of the town, who did not, however, seem much interested in my remarks.

"The next morning the king again endeavored to stop me, by refusing guides, on the plea that there was war in the direction in which I wished to go, and whoever went with me, might get into trouble. This I well knew was false, and I told him so; but to no purpose. Indignant at so flagrant a breach of faith, I immediately issued orders to prepare for our return home. Just as my bag, umbrella and stick were brought out of the hut, the unprincipled old king, who had walked off in high dudgeon, returned, and learning the state of affairs, at once gave his consent. Forthwith, two young men, unmindful of the dangers of the way, which a moment before were so formidable, offered their services as guides, and

in five minutes we left the village and struck a bush
path leading in a northwest direction. The country was
covered with a low bush, which became higher and more
entangled as we advanced. The vines and boughs pro-
jecting over the path, hung down in our faces, while the
high grass, which completely concealed the road, obliged
us to wade as though walking through snow. Under
such circumstances, travelling could not be otherwise
than laborious in the extreme. No one appeared to have
made use of the path before us, except an unlucky wight
whom we met leading a refractory cow and calf, and
who informed us that he had passed the preceding
night in the forest. The truth of this was afterwards
confirmed to us, though we are still unable to guess by
what means he managed to protect himself and his cow
from the wild beasts.

"About eight o'clock, we entered a majestic, but
gloomy forest, which, to all appearance, had never, since
creation, yielded to the hand of man. Here were no
overhanging boughs and no grass, but the path, if path
it could be called, was impeded by the bodies of enormous trees, which lay across it. To one who has never
visited the tropics, it would be in vain to attempt to give
an adequate idea of the African forests; so enormous are
the trees; so impervious is the shade. The atmosphere,
in these forests, is very close, causing the traveller to
perspire profusely, and of course inducing intense thirst.
Frequently during the day, we crossed fine, bold streams,
as clear as chrystal, tumbling over the rocks, or rushing
over beds of gravel. Sorely was I tempted to stoop
and quaff the delicious draught, but dire experience had

taught me the impropriety of such a course. The strict-
est temperance, in both eating and drinking, is necessary, if we expect to escape those terrible diseases to
which African travellers are so liable, and which have
so often thwarted the best planned expeditions.

"We had no time-piece with us, and, of course, could
not speak accurately as to the time consumed in crossing
this gloomy forest, save that, although we moved at a
rapid rate, many a long hour elapsed ere we reached
its northern boundary. Winding our way through the
long grass of a deserted rice field, we reached the top of
a lofty hill. Here a scene of surpassing beauty was presented to our view. An immense valley, hemmed in on
either side by conical hills, clothed with luxuriant vegetation, lay at our feet. The sun, now rapidly declining
in the heavens, lent additional splendor to the land-
scape.

"But my thoughts were far otherwise engaged than
in admiring the view. In that beautiful valley dwelt
the Krebbo, and all the tales which I had heard of their
cruelty and cannabalism, now rushed on my mind, and
awakened impressions far from pleasant; but there was
no retreat. We advanced, and in a few moments were
in their farms and among the dreaded race. Instead,
however, of ferocious savages, we saw a people more
mild and gentle than those whom we had just left.
Learning that the headman of the next village was on
a neighboring farm, we sent for him. After some delay,
a withered looking little old man made his appearance,
who, we were informed, was the most renowned of the
Krebbo; but whether this renown had been gained by

deeds of valor, or was merely consequent upon the possession of wealth, did not appear; probably, the latter.
I stated, in few words the object of my visit, letting him
know, at the same time, that I had brought no valua-
bles with me. He expressed himself pleased to see me,
and invited me to stay at his town; but we were afterwards informed that he vented his displeasure in no
very measured terms, feeling himself deeply aggrieved
that I should visit him and not bring the wherewithal
to pay for my entertaintment. My experience had
taught me that a white man and his money were considered, in Africa, as fair game, and that his trouble
would frequently be in proportion to the amount of his
possessions. On this account, I had ventured on the
somewhat hazardous experiment of going without any
money at all. Under such circumstances, robbery was
impossible; for, to an African, brown linen jackets and
trowsers are of small value; nor would there be the
same inducement to impede my progress from one tribe
to another, inasmuch as they would gain nothing by
detaining me, and even a cannibal would turn, with
despair, from a carcass so attenuated as mine. After
some delay, the old man sent me something to eat.

" The next day being the Sabbath, of course we did
not travel, and not wishing to trespass too much on the
hospitality of my host, I declined receiving any thing but
rice; an arrangement far from agreeable to my attendants. My hut was thronged by the towns people, who
came to gaze upon the white man. Among the rest
was my host, who, watching his opportunity when the
hut was nearly vacant, asked me whether I could read

a book? I replied by requesting to see it, when, shut-
ting the door, he drew forth, from the bottom of a chest,
a volume carefully wrapped in grass, which, on examination, I found to be a Bible, published by the ' Society
for the Promotion of Christian Knowledge.' By his own
account, he had received it from a man on the coast in
return for ivory, probably under the impression that it
was a most potent greegree. He objected to lending
me the book, lest his people should become aware of its
being in his possession, but consented, on being reminded
that every one seeing it in my hands would suppose it to
be mine. There was no writing in the book whereby to
infer its history with any certainty. In all probability it
was given by some well meaning, though misjudging
person, in Sierra Leone, to a Krooman, who used it to
impose on the credulity of this old man. Meeting with
it where I did, was like unexpectedly welcoming an old
friend.

"The greater part of the day was occupied in conversing with them on religious matters, and, in the evening I preached to as many as would come to hear me."

CHAPTER XX.

THIS paper is evidently left unfinished, and we have no account of his homeward journey, but Mrs. Minor writes : " Upon his return, such was the exposure and fatigue to which he had been subjected, that when he suddenly entered the room, all drenched with rain, I rose to bid the stranger welcome, for I knew him not. It was easily seen that his visit had made an impression upon the natives, and that the being who had thus visited their country and home, was an object of interest to them ; for they flocked to Mt. Vaughan to inquire for ' Minor,' as they called him—' that white man who one time came to their country and talked God-palaver to them,' bringing him presents, and inviting him to come again. Upon these occasions, Mr. Minor generally carried a gun, for sport, rather than as a weapon. He could out-walk any native man he ever met with, as they freely acknowledged themselves, saying, ' Minor pass native man too much, that time he go in the bush.' His love for his brother missionaries was strong, even unto death, and, in all cases of peril and danger, his language was—' here I am, send me. My life is immortal till my work is done.' His moral

or Christian courage, his most prominent trait of character, caused the natives to say : 'True, Minor be God-man,
but he be war-man too, that time he shoot at monkey or
bird, he never miss his mark, it be sure to fall.' In all
cases where conscience was not involved. he adopted the
fashions and customs of the people, partaking of their
food when hospitably offered him. He loved Africa as
his adopted home, and the novel and exciting life which
he was obliged to lead among the natives. Upon one
occasion, at the house of the Rev. Mr. Wilson, it was
playfully said to him, 'as for you, Mr. Minor, you should
be sent back to labor in America, you would then feel
what self-denial is.' 'True enough,' said he, 'it is even
so.' His interest in some Indian tribes when in the
West, before going to Africa, prepared him, no doubt, in
some degree, for his mission."

It was in the autumn of 1841, that the missionary
brethren resolved upon opening a station without the
bounds of the Maryland Colony. To Mr. Minor the
way now seemed opened for the fulfilment of his long
cherished desire to devote himself entirely to the natives,
and he volunteered his services for an exploring expedi-
tion. We will give the result in his own words.

"The inhabitants of that region, Taboo, who call
themselves Plabo, had more than once expressed to Dr.
Savage, during several visits to that place, a strong
desire for a school, and the opening appearing favorable
and opportune, the brethren advised that I should visit
and examine the spot. They yielded with little difficulty, promising to give up to us a hill back of the town,
occupied as a burying place. They agreed, moreover,

to clear it of bush, and erect for us a native house, where we might live whilst building a more permanent one for ourselves. All this was to be entirely gratis. During the parley, almost the whole assembly visited the top of the hill; with the exception of a small part, it was densely covered with trees, interwoven from top to bottom with vines of every size and shape, forming one mass of verdure. The king made a speech on the occasion, to the dead, addressed more particularly to the body of some great man which lay on an elevated platform. He begged him not to regard what they were about to do as an insult, as the ground was not for themselves, but for God and a white man who was coming to reside in their country; a thing he and his fathers had desired greatly, but had not seen. A neighboring town, actuated by jealousy, offered some opposition, which was speedily overruled. I returned home without giving them a decided answer, but promised they should hear from us shortly.

"My report coinciding with Dr. Savage's, as regarded the eligibility of the spot, the brethren instructed me to take steps immediately for opening a station there. A messenger was dispatched to inform the people, and direct them to clear the ground and erect the house as soon as possible, which they promised to do, and send us word when completed. A month elapsed, and we hearing nothing from them, dispatched another messenger, to see what was the matter. In due time he returned and reported, that not a stick had been touched, the people giving as an excuse, that they were afraid the white man was only playing with them ;

8

however, being assured by our messenger, they turned
out in a body, and cleared off a considerable space,
promising to erect the house forthwith. Not feeling
satisfied, I deemed it advisable to go in person, and
found them preparing to remove a house, from the town
to the hill we were to occupy. A spot of ground had
been cleared, it is true, but the top of the hill and the
burying ground remained as they were. Demanding
why they had not fulfilled their promises, they declared
they were afraid, particularly of the man on the elevated
platform, who, when living, was remarkable for his vin-
dictive character, and they doubted not he retained the
same disposition still. They at length agreed, however,
that if I would take the responsibility on my own shoul-
ders of cutting the first bush, they would follow suit. To
this agreement there was no objection, so grasping a
cullup, without more adieu, I laid about me manfully,
and to do them justice, they were not slow to follow. In
the course of three hours, a considerable space was
cleared, and the king proposed they should go for the
house : it was acceded to, and after taking some re-
freshment, the whole body adjourned to a small town
where stood the house to be removed. Their plan was
to remove the house-top, entire, which was nearly equivalent to the whole house, and had they done so, they
would have saved themselves much trouble. Half the
number present might have carried it with ease, had
they worked to advantage ; but there was no order,
none to command, or rather all commanded ; a few
would exhaust their strength in vain efforts, while others
stood by, utterly regardless of their clamorous cries for

assistance. At last it started, and went on very well, until reaching a slight ascent, some difficulty occurred ; each ran to save himself, regardless of his neighbor— several were caught under it, as in a trap, but fortunately only one was injured ; three times was the same scene repeated, and each time some were more or less injured. The difficulties arose from their utter lack of faith in each other, each one being under the constant apprehension that his companions would run away and leave him to be crushed. After many vexatious delays, the house was almost completed, and I was given to understand that payment was expected, though in the first instance, there had been a distinct understanding to the contrary. I had been too long acquainted with the African mode of transacting business to be easily surprised, but the enormity of the demand was certainly far beyond anything that previous experience would have led me to expect. It was of course met by a prompt refusal. This was but one attempt to defraud me ; in all our transactions they exhibited the same want of faith, as a most prominent trait. There was not one among the negociators who hesitated to tell the most barefaced falsehood, if thereby he could obtain the slightest advantage, and in no one case, did they manifest a disposition to act fairly."

CHAPTER XXI.

Notes descriptive of his mode of life at Taboo, addressed by Mr Minor to his wife.

FROM the commencement of this undertaking, Mr. Minor spent most of his time at Taboo, living in a native hut and in native style, and only visiting Mt. Vaughan once a month, to attend the business meetings of the missionaries. His journeys were generally made on foot, and it is believed that these exertions, as well as the deprivations and fatigue incident to the opening of his new station, tended greatly to undermine his health. A graphic picture of his mode of life at this time, is furnished in the notes which he addressed to Mrs. Minor, who still remained at Mt. Vaughan during these intervals of absence. They tell such an unvarnished tale of the discomforts and trials of actual missionary life, that we believe they will be useful in dispelling the romantic associations too often thrown around this work; and they cannot fail to be interesting, as presenting a faithful view of the spirit in which their discomforts and trials were met by the writer.

Many of them are without date, and the extracts can, therefore, be arranged only by conjecture. The following was written at Rockbookah, a few miles below Cavalla:

"My dear Mary,—We are safe thus far on our way, thank God! When we reached the landing, at Sheppard's Lake, the canoe was gone, and the natives say H. Harmon took it ; so we *waded* the lake, and *walked* the beach with our *heavy* load. —— —— is low spirited : most of the boys are away. Brother Appleby is going to Taboo with me.

"Good-bye, my dear Mary. God watch over and keep you."

"Taboo, —— —, —.

"Though my messenger will not go farther than Cavalla, I cannot forbear dropping you a line, to say how much I miss you. I have been the greater part of to-day, looking out for timber, which is plentiful, but not of the kind I want.

"I shot two pigeons and one monkey, which we will eat, now *you* are not here. The king has just expressed a hope that you will come soon, that he may fall heir to all the monkeys I kill. Take care of yourself, my dear wife."

"Taboo, *October* 12th, 1841.

"My Dear Wife :—I have determined to send a messenger to Mr. Appleby to-morrow, for a grindstone, and, of course, could not let him go without a note to you. We have commenced house-keeping in grand style. I eat what I can get, chickens, crabs, monkeys, hawks, and kill crows for the boys. I have enclosed and dug up a spot of ground for a garden—the nucleus of a larger one, I hope. There are now planted in it

potatoes, tomatoes, oranges, ginger, &c. The tomatoes
and potatoes will live, I hope. Brother Appleby is here
with me, and we make our own bread, which is sour,
by-the-bye. Things get on tolerably well with me. The
dysentery has reached us at last. Take care of yourself,
my dear wife, and pray for your husband.

" L. B. Minor."

" Brother Appleby leaves me to-morrow; I should
be glad if he would stay longer, but he cannot. The
dysentery is spreading; the people of the town are engaged, to-day, in ' making fetish,' to keep it off. The
king has ' dashed ' Brother Appleby a kid, which we
will eat to-day. I wish you could have a part. Send
me bread whenever you can, it is better for me, just
now, than rice. A ship passed to-day, and took off
some of my men. J. Stone is quite at home, and rather
too fond of going to town, which, however, I have forbidden."

" Taboo, October 13th.

" Though I have commenced house-keeping and sit at
my own table every day, yet my situation is very far from
being comfortable. From morning until night, my hut
is filled with natives of every age, jabbering incessantly.
Could the time be employed in religious conversation, I
would not object, but this is seldom within my power.
There is one indefatigable student among them, however. He learned all his letters last Sunday, and is
now spelling,

" My operations are going on tolerably well. Quite

a large spot of ground has been cleared, and I am now preparing to run a partition across my hut, where I may enjoy a little privacy—a luxury I can have at no time, under present circumstances."

"TABOO, *November* 7th, 1841.

"I had expected to despatch a messenger this morning to Cavalla, and, possibly, to Mt. Vaughan, but have been disappointed in consequence of the people having obtained a turtle; and, of course, none are willing to be absent from the feast. The major part are keeping holiday, or, as they term it, 'Sunday,' in honor of the occasion. * * * * * * * *

"The bread is not yet exhausted and keeps well. I only wish that I had more—it is a great help.

"Congregation, yesterday, good—all could not get into the house. Preaching next Sunday in the open air, weather permitting."

"TABOO, *November* —, 1841.

"Last Monday night I was bitten by a centipede. It gave me a good deal of pain, but the immediate application of remedies brought relief. I am now, thank God, quite recovered.

"My house is still much thronged by natives, otherwise, I might be tolerably comfortable."

"TABOO, *November* 24th, 1841.

"Though there is, at present, no opportunity of sending a letter, I have seated myself at the table to write, in order to have a long letter ready, when one does occur. There is little of interest to relate. Most of the people are, at this moment, stupid with palm wine, and Peter is lying in my back room, dead drunk; brought home, in that state, by John, a few moments since. A native man is now seated in my house making baskets, after our fashion, under my direction. He has nearly completed two. The second, quite large and handsome. One, the first, is made for the Doctor—the second, and largest, is for you. I have been much troubled with nervous depression since I left you the last time. My poor mother suffers from it much, and mine, probably, will be a similar lot. The notes and papers were received last night and carefully perused, not excepting the ' Luminary.' "

" *December* 15th, 1841.

" Jackson goes up to-morrow, and takes one of my sick men with him ; the other is too weak yet to walk so far. My own health is not good. I have been much harrassed getting timber out of the bush, and not half is out yet. I have no tea or coffee, and little else besides palm oil and rice to eat. I have not time to go out with my gun. The carpenters, I presume, buy the fowls ; I have only bought two since I came down. The boys are well, but do not learn, for I have no time to teach them   I hope you are better off for something to eat than I am; but do not suppose that I lay this to heart. To-morrow I will try to shoot something.

" Good bye, my dearest Mary."

" Hardy goes up to-morrow, which leaves me without a carpenter. The timber for the house is almost all out of the bush. My health, thank God! is pretty good just now, but my living, very poor. Had the carpenters remained, I did not expect to have been with you until Christmas-eve, but as they will not stay, I shall have nothing to detain me so long; though I cannot say, just now, what day I shall be up; but this is certain, that it will be as soon as consistent with duty. J. Stone will go up with Hardy, in order that he may be present at Communion. Try to help him to be ready."

" *Clouds!* Two carpenters sick, and another gone home. The natives had a palaver among themselves, and say they are afraid to go into the bush to work, and I, myself, am not well. Great exertion will be necessary, on my part, to keep them from coming to a dead stand. Jackson had stopped for want of timber. If you can spare it well, send some tea and coffee. Ask the Doctor to send some more cough medicine, as my cold still holds on. I shall have no dinner to-day, in order to let my cook go after timber. I met with no hindrance on the beach, but on the contrary, the kindest treatment. I know not why my faith should be so weak, I have had many mercies. If I only could get some Irish potatoes, I might get on tolerably well. Let the bearer have thirty-six small blue-edged plates."

Such requests as this often occur in these notes. It was in such articles, crockery, handkerchiefs, tobacco, &c., that the workmen were paid, and it was, at this time, considered unsafe to keep many goods on hand, lest the natives should be excited to plunder.

8*

In one of his notes about this time occurs the following passage, illustrative of the superstitious character of the people, and their belief in the influence of departed spirits. He writes, " The dysentery does not appear quite so rife as it was. Thank God for it ! as otherwise, they might have attributed it to my clearing up the burying ground."

" DEAREST MARY,—Your note was received last night. When I know you are well and happy, I am content to remain here ; but it is a very different thing when you are not well. I then do nothing but think of your lonely condition. * * * * * * *

" I look upon your coming here just now as utterly out of the question. By the help of God, I will not turn from toil or danger myself, but subjecting you to it is another matter. I cannot and will not do it.

" My garden is nearly enclosed with a fence that will be good when we are dead. God bless you !

" Your affectionate husband,

" L. B. MINOR."

The following appears to have been written after his return from one of his monthly journeys to Mt. Vaughan :

" TABOO, *March 20th*, 1842.

" I am here safe, though I had some trouble on the way. The people at the Cavalla River would not let me have a canoe without paying a most exorbitant sum ; so I had to retrace my weary way along the hot

and heavy sand-beach to Brother Smith's, where, with
some difficulty and considerable expense, I got a canoe,
which took me by sea to Rockbookah. It was a small
canoe, and somewhat broken, so that I got very wet;
indeed, sat in the water. My clothes and bread were
wetted with salt water. I arrived here at midnight,
much fatigued."

"TABOO, *August 9th*, 1842.

"DEAREST MARY,—Your note has just reached me,
and was opened with a trembling hand, fearing greatly
it might be the messenger of evil, though I was somewhat relieved by seeing your hand-writing on the back.

"I am painfully anxious about you, more so than
becomes a Christian, but can only pray for you. We
cannot hope to be long here. God grant we may be
ready when our Father sends for us !

"I do not think the prospect so bright as when I
left here, but have hope. Since writing to you last,
several have offered to work, but all must leave when
their rice is ripe. They have been employed in clearing
away around the house, and working the garden. We
are sadly off for plates, mugs, &c.—indeed, for almost
everything. I hear the Doctor will be down—if so, tell
him that for his own good, he had better come prepared
with bread, butter, &c. I have tomatoes in abundance,
and should have had potatoes if the cows and goats
would have permitted me. John wants some small
needles and patches.

"Much love to Mr. and Mrs. Payne."

" *September 4th,* 1842.

" Your note, received last Saturday, removed a load
from my breast. I was apprehensive that some evil
might come to you from the palaver, but had not sufficient ground on which to act—a state of suspense more
painful than I can well describe. This constant separation from you, I cannot bear. I was joined to you for
better and for worse; and certainly, as you are now,
you might as well have no husband. If you were in
America, and among your friends, it would be another
matter, but here, in this country of palaver and trouble,
for you to be left without any one to supply your wants,
or attend properly to you in sickness, and protect you in
time of danger, will not do. Thank God! the time of
our reunion is near at hand, I hope! *   *   *   *   *
I cannot say what day I can leave; but when I can, I
will fly to you ' as doves to their windows.' The congregations on Sunday are larger than ever, and things
look encouraging. May God give me grace to be faithful and zealous! *   *   *   * We are about to begin
Musu's house. I wish Jack to come down and bring my
cow, and, if you can spare him, Elisha.

" God bless you, my own dear Mary.

                              " Yours most truly."

Some hesitation was felt about inserting the following note, but the very minuteness of its details will
assist the reader in forming a vivid conception of the
circumstances of the writer.

" We are here, at Taboo, without accident, thank

God! and have been very kindly received by the inhabitants. Gray goes up to-morrow, and is to carry this note ; if he returns immediately, please send by him, the little tea-kettle the Doctor was to let me have, and also fifty flints, which you will find upstairs on the cot, done up in brown paper. I feel rather lonely, and have no book but the Bible, the best I could have. Wrap up the flints in Churchman or a Recorder; it will do to read some odd time. I shall write to the Doctor : for the present, farewell !"

Then by way of postcript he adds : " Send me a piece of beef, well wrapt up. Please send me a comb, a bottle of strained oil, and some salt, put up in a jar."

CHAPTER XXII.

Outrage committed by the Natives at Little Bereby.—Letter to the Hon. Abel P. Upshur.—Extracts from Mr. Minor's Journal.

THE above correspondence presents to us a view of the ordinary trials to which Mr. Minor was exposed during this year of toil and privation, but it makes no reference to the imminent peril in which he was placed by the circumstances detailed in the following letter.

" *To the* HON. ABEL P. UPSHUR, *Secretary to the U. S. Navy.*

" TABOO, WEST AFRICA, ⎫
" *Lat.* 4° 40. *Long.* 5° 20. *April 25th* 1842. ⎭

" SIR,—The subject of this letter will, I hope, sufficiently account for my boldness in addressing you, and occupying time, of which every moment must be precious. Yesterday, within thirty miles of the place from which I now write, a bloody tragedy was enacted ; and as it was American blood that was spilt, wantonly and without provocation, real or pretended, I feel it an imperative duty to lay the matter before you ; the more, that I am the only white man near the spot, left alive to tell the horrid tale. The facts of the case are as follows. Captain Farwell, of the Schooner Mary Car-

ver, Boston, was at a town east of this place, called
Little Bereby or Half Bereby, where he had deposited
some goods in the hands of a native called Young Cracow, for the purchase of camwood. Having occasion to
be absent a short time, and on his return not finding the
wood ready, he proposed that a canoe should be given
him in part payment, to which Cracow, after some hesitation, agreed. The canoe was received in lieu of
six hundred pounds of camwood, a large price. The
captain, apprehending no danger, was enticed on shore,
and while amused with a pretence of trade, his boat
and several canoes, all loaded with camwood, were sent
to the schooner. The mate, suspecting no harm, allowed all hands to come on board, and while engaged
in weighing the wood, was suddenly set upon. He, one
seaman, and the cook were the first who fell. One seaman, a very old man, was thrown overboard, and the
only remaining hand, having taken refuge in the rigging,
was induced by fair promises, to surrender, and instantly
butchered. At a preconcerted signal, the captain, till
then unconscious of what had been going on, was seized,
bound hand and foot, and cruelly beaten. The women
struck him so severely with their rice-pestles that his
scull was fractured just above the eye, causing it to
protrude from the socket in a manner horrible to behold.
He begged for time to pray. It was refused. He was
then taken out to sea in a canoe, and thrown overboard,
bound as he was. Still, the unhappy man struggled
for his life with all the energy of desperation, and succeeded in tearing, with his teeth, the cords with which
his hands were bound, and even seized a paddle to de-

fend himself, but a blow on the head sent him to the bottom.

"Accustomed as the natives are to blacken the character of those they have injured, in the present case, they have nothing to allege against their victim. They do not even pretend to have disagreed with him in any manner. They glory in what they have done. It is said that this is the fourth vessel cut off at that place, (I know certainly of two, one Brazilian and one American,) within the last eight months. The kroomen and trademen, serving on board at the time, participated largely, both in the murders and in the plunder.

"It would ill become me, a minister of the Gospel, to recommend any unnecessary effusion of blood, but forbearance, in the present case, would not be mercy. It would be evident to every one acquainted with the African character, that a severe example is now absolutely necessary, to secure any thing like respect and security to our countrymen trading on the coast. Should this outrage be overlooked, the effect not only there, but all along the coast, would be pernicious in the highest degree. This very morning, I saw the people of two towns near this place, (one of them in sight of the spot from which I write,) going to attack a Dutch ship at anchor, the captain of which was, by their own admission, a kind and liberal man. Timely notice enabled the Dutchman to escape; but they may yet take a bloody revenge on me, for the part I took in conveying the warning.

"There is, in the minds of many in America, and more especially in England, an over-wrought sensibility with regard to the African race, which leads them to repre-

hend, in the strongest manner, the infliction of any punishment, however well deserved. Believe me sir, this
is a mistaken kindness. My knowledge of the African
character has not been gained among those who, having
resided long among the whites, have adopted, in a
greater or less degree, the views and habits of civilized
society; nor on shipboard, where the power of the white
man is undisputed, and where there is every motive to
practise those arts of deception for which they are so
distinguished. Under such circumstances, the more
mischievous features of their character are rarely seen.
My knowledge has been acquired in their villages, in
their huts, where no motives for concealment existed,
and where their sentiments are freely expressed; where
their heart, throwing aside its disguise, appears in all its
native hideousness. I hesitate not, therefore, to assert,
that until better motives can be supplied, nothing but
the fear of punishment, promptly and sharply administered, will restrain their lawless violence; outrage will
follow outrage, and deriving courage from impunity,
each case will outdo its predecessor. By severity, is not
meant the mere burning of the town. That is nothing.
Were Little Bereby to-day reduced to ashes, one-tenth
of the plunder obtained from the schooner would be sufficient to restore it to a better condition than ever. The
course pursued at Qualla Batto affords an example of
what might be done here, with advantage. The anchor-
age and landing at Bereby are both good, and the town,
being neither large nor strong, might be easily surrounded in the night, and destroyed in an hour: but
great secrecy will be necessary in approaching the coast,

for should the inhabitants have but an hour's notice, not one will be found, and news passes along the coast with amazing celerity.

"Should you need more precise information with regard to the localities, I beg leave to refer you to Captain R. E. Lawlin, New-York, and to Captain T. Hunt, Salem, Massachusetts.

"I remain, very respectfully,
"Your obedient servant,
"L. B. Minor,
"*Missionary of the Episcopal Church.*"

That the apprehensions expressed in this letter were not unfounded, is evident from a subsequent notice of the affair in his correspondence with the Committee. Under date of July 4th, he writes: "We have since learned, from more than one source, that part of the original plan was to murder me; not that they had aught against me, or would gain any thing thereby, but to prevent the possibility of my giving information. Repeatedly has the letter of the Dutchman been thrown in my teeth, and as often have I avowed that I would again do the same, should a like occasion offer; yet has not our Heavenly Father suffered a hair of our heads to be harmed, nor is our peace in any way marred, for our trust is in Him."

A short journal, commencing August 15th, is the only subsequent record from his own pen.

"For some time past, there has been, evidently, more than usual readiness to hear and receive the truth of the Gospel, but nothing decisive took place till within a few days past. Last Saturday I walked round, as usual, to give notice of the approaching Sabbath, and spoke pointedly to several. The next morning I was agreeably surprised to hear that all the men of the town had remained at home, and were coming to hear God palaver. This was good news indeed, and for it, I failed not to thank God fervently; earnestly praying for grace to meet the occasion aright, for his glory. My discourse was on the importance and necessity of observing the Sabbath, reminding them that, in days gone by, they were ignorant, but that now God had sent one across the wide waters to teach them what was right, he certainly would expect them to receive and obey his laws. After service the king and headmen remarked, that all that had been said was reasonable; that no one could work all the time; that God was their Father and should be obeyed, and many other remarks of like import. Every thing wore a most favorable aspect, when a troublesome fellow abruptly demanded why I did not do as the other God-men did; and went on to say that Mr. Payne and the new God-men (Romanists,) paid people to keep Sunday. Gain is, at all times, the most exciting topic that can possibly be presented to the native mind, and did not fail of its effects on this occasion, as was very apparent. I, however, went on to assure them that they were entirely mistaken with regard to Mr. Payne, who had never given any thing of the kind; and though the new God-men had given a hogshead of tobacco for that purpose, it had been of no avail, for after using it, the people broke the Sabbath as much as ever;

and if they kept the Sabbath for hire, it would not be acceptable to God, who had already given them so many good things; at the same time enumerating those most apparent. 'All those,' replied one, ' he gave us when we followed our old customs, which you wish us to give up.' 'Yes,' I replied, ' our heavenly Father is too kind to suffer even his disobedient children to starve, but this is certainly no reason why we should continue to disobey him.'

"Here the interpreter, Musu, a fine young man, of whom I shall speak hereafter, took up the matter in an animated discussion, strenuously advocating my side of the question. A sharp conversation followed, while I prayed that truth might prevail. I found soon, that more were on my side, or rather on God's side, than against Him. Finally, the two first objectors said they were willing to keep Sunday, but wished me to do something to please them. 'Had nothing been done?' I replied. 'Is it nothing to leave home and kindred, and come to teach you, without emolument or reward; and have not you received many presents at our hands, and have not you, R. and W.,' addressing the two first objectors, 'been partakers of those presents?' One hung down his head, but the other, more bold, was about to reply, when he was silenced by the almost unanimous voice of those present, the king declaring that they made him ' ashamed.' Many were for passing a law to keep Sunday, on the spot; others objected, and not thinking them yet prepared for so bold a step, I did not urge it. The Kroomen who were present, remarked that at Cape Coast, Sierra Leone, and other places where they had

been, and where white men live, the people of the country, after awhile, left off their own ' fash,' and turned to
do ' white man's fash ;' and gave it as their opinion, that
such would be the case here by and by.

" *August 20th.*—To-day, while in conversation with
Kraplo, the king, he expressed it as his firm opinion, that
his father, who, he doubts not, is in heaven, was the
means of influencing God to send me here to teach him
and his people. If his representations are to be trusted,
his father must have been an extraordinary man. Many
of his precepts, as reported, are such as would have done
honor to Socrates; all unite in saying he was celebrated
as a peacemaker.

" *August 21st.*—God has certainly blessed me in
giving me such an interpreter as Musu, the man alluded
to above. From the first, he attached himself to me,
and served me with such zeal that I feared he would
soon wear out, but so far from this being the case, his
zeal has increased. All who have seen him, both missionaries and colonists, agree in saying that he differs
from any native they have met with ; and, what is most
remarkable, never since his connection with me, have I
had cause to suspect him of falsehood ; and never, but
once, of defrauding me of a pin's value, and then, he
subsequently cleared up the whole affair to my perfect
satisfaction. There is indeed good reason to hope that
a work of grace is begun in his heart, he having openly
renounced all the objectionable customs of his country,
and when his old father, who is more disposed to engraft
Christianity on Heathenism, than to renounce any part
of his present creed, killed a bullock for the devil, he

would not take a morsel of it, or join in any of the ceremonies, though repeatedly urged to do so, and all, too,
when I was absent. He learns with great facility, and
we all humbly hope and pray, that he may, in time, become a messenger of peace to his heathen countrymen.
He is about twenty-two years of age, and has but one
wife, whom he tries hard to bring round to his views.

    " *August 22d.*—Congregation, yesterday, better than
ever, though it is the height of the rice harvest. God
enable me to address them with more than usual free-
dom ; some women attended, and were very attentive.

    " *August 29th.*—Congregation, yesterday, still larger ;
many women, but my sermon was not attended with
that unction from above which it should have been.
Resolved, with the help of God, to observe every Friday
as a day of fasting and prayer, with a special reference
to my labors on Saturday and Sunday.

    " *August 30th.*—Heard to-day of a movement at
Brother Payne's, touching the Sabbath, and also at
Brother Appleby's, which seems likely to end in something decidedly in favor of the observance of that holy
day. God in mercy grant that it may be the dawn of a
brighter day to us !"

CHAPTER XXIII.

Mr. Minor's declining health—His last illness and death.

WE have abundantly remarked that Mr. Minor's health was evidently injured by his long and laborious journies, and by the privations and toil encountered at Taboo, in the establishment of his Station. In January, 1843, he removed his family to their new home ; but now that he had attained the very position which he had so long desired, and the way seemed opened for the vigorous prosecution of the work he so much loved, his friends watched, with anxious solicitude, the ravages of disease upon his already enfeebled frame. He had been, for several months, troubled with repeated attacks of diarrhœa, a disease to which he was constitutionally subject, and which, he had often said, would probably be the cause of his death. He, however, continued to preach to good congregations, and to attend to the other duties of the Station until about the middle of March, when he was obliged to inform the people that he was too sick to talk " God-palaver" to them any more, at present, but hoped soon to be able to resume his labors. He had already gained a strong hold upon their affections, and much regret was expressed for his illness. " What for," they would say, " God send a God-man to us, and then make

him sick? We no sabby that." They were told that
they had not obeyed the instructions of their teacher, and
perhaps God was punishing them for the abuse of his
gifts, by their withdrawal. "True," they replied, "that
be true enough—my heart tell me that be true; 'spose
he die, think God send another God-man?"

About this time, Doctor Savage advised a sea
voyage, but the only American captain on the coast refused to have a sick man on board his vessel, and no
other opportunity occurred. When Mr. Minor received
the note communicating this denial, he read it with emotion, and laid it down without a word. Mrs. Minor remarked, "You are disappointed." "Yes," he replied,
"but no doubt all is for the best."

On the 21st of April, he was so much worse, that he
expressed his belief that he could not recover, and desired that his brethren might be informed of his situation. He also commenced a farewell letter to his mother,
which seems to have been abruptly terminated—probably owing to his weakness; but which, short as it is,
comprehends all that her bereaved heart would most
desire—the assurance of undying love and triumphant
faith.

"MY DEAREST MOTHER,—The time is approaching
when this flesh will return to the dust; but I know
that my Redeemer liveth. I am too weak to write to
you, dearest mother, but I shall welcome you at the
right hand of God."

On the 22d, he was visited by the Rev. Mr. Smith,

and Dr. Savage arrived the next day. He was much relieved by the remedies administered, and when visited on the 5th of May by Mr. and Mrs. Payne, appeared decidedly better. He continued to improve until the 16th, when he was removed to Cavalla, where he expired on the 29th of May, 1843, aged 29 years. The particulars of his illness and death will, however, be best learned from an account, written at the time, by the Rev. Dr. Savage. It is as follows :

" Mr. Minor's health had been declining for some months. About February, he was put upon a regular course of medicine, with evident benefit. I advised him to avail himself of the first opportunity for a voyage at sea. No such opportunity occurring, he gradually grew worse, and on the 21st of April, a severe diarrhœa supervened. In his then feeble state, nothing but danger could be apprehended from such an occurrence. I proceeded immediately to his station upon being informed of his case, and found him dangerously sick, with a full conviction upon his mind that he could not recover. No anxiety was visible, however, respecting the result, but he seemed to be calm, peaceful and resigned. The exercises of his mind during this attack were interesting and gratifying to his friends.

" Among my remedies, was opium, administered in large, continued doses, at short intervals. Under its influence, he was inclined to sleep, and, at times, to stupor ; hence, he was much incapacitated for connected thought. But, awaking from sleep, he would have moments of clearness, and request me to pray, expressing great pleasure in the exercise. On one such occasion he re-

9

marked, 'Prayer is sweet—we ought to pray more. Were we more earnest for ourselves, our interpreters, and our people, we should be more successful.

"He frequently expressed a sense of his unworthiness and unprofitableness, declaring the atonement of Christ to be the only ground of his acceptance before God. In the course of conversation on this point he said, 'Oh, Doctor, I am a sinner, a sinner saved by grace.' Soon after this, waking from sleep, he said, 'I had sweet thoughts of Christ—oh! he *is* my Saviour.' Usually, he left it with me to suggest the points of request in prayer, but on one occasion, he said, 'Pray that I may have patience.'

"At one time, he seemed to have considerable anxiety about the continuance and prosperity of his station in case of his immediate death, and affectingly asked, 'Who will take my place?' I could only say, 'God will provide—can you not leave it to him?' He did not refer to the subject again.

"There was a time when his case appeared to be very doubtful, and I informed him that the probability was decidedly against him. He proceeded, with great calmness, exhibiting much conscientiousness in so doing, to give directions concerning his private affairs and his station, expressing his desire that neither individuals nor the Mission should lose anything through his management. His request, often repeated, was, 'Let all payments be liberally made.' His disease was peculiarly obstinate, and on one occasion, I informed him that if it did not soon yield, he must die. He replied, 'Let it be as God directs. I have no desire to live, but to benefit others.' Soon after, his case took a favorable turn, and on the ninth day after my arrival, I left him in an advanced stage of convalescence. It was decided that I should return in a week, to accompany him up to my station, where he could be immediately under my attention, and the more readily take advantage of an opportunity for a trip to sea. On the arrival of the appointed time, I felt too unwell to do it, and requested Mr. Payne to go down for that purpose. He was accompanied by Mr. Smith, who went to remain with Mrs. Minor till she could complete her arrangements for the contemplated absence. They found Mr. Minor able to walk about, though very feeble. They left Taboo on the 16th of May, at two o'clock P. M., (Mr. Minor reclining in a travelling basket,) and arrived at Cavalla, Mr. Payne's station, at about ten the same evening; a distance of twenty-five miles. On arriving, he felt fatigued, and went immediately to bed. Next day, his disease returned. Finding it did not yield to remedies, I was sent for, and arrived on the 18th. His symptoms I found of the most alarming character. Under a vigorous use of remedies, they were, for a time, kept at bay, and through the following day his case bore a decidedly favorable aspect. On the third day, Saturday, a change for the worse took place. His nervous system was greatly disordered, and he would call up long absent and distant objects to his mind. Among the most prominent, and one upon which he delighted to dwell, was the image of his aged mother, for whom he had retained an unabated affection.

"At night his wife arrived in company with Mr.

Smith. He indulged freely in inquiries about persons and things at his station, and seemed to be a good deal excited. The night was one of great restlessness, and the next day, Sunday, he was much worse. From that time, no amendment was perceptible, but, on the contrary, an aggravation of his symptoms and gradual progress of disease. I now made known to him my opinion that he would not recover—that his end was approaching. The announcement seemed to cause no surprise. The calmness and peace of mind before apparent, were still undisturbed. I asked him again respecting his hopes of salvation, in view of his present nearness to eternity. His reply was of the same tenor. Faith in the atonement of Christ was the doctrine he had preached—that by which he had lived, and that upon which his soul rested, now that he was about to die. Previously, he had requested the frequent prayers of his brethren, but, from this time, he became absorbed in the exercise himself. I asked him to remember in his supplications the Mission, and his associates, and myself in particular. He replied, in an emphatic manner, 'I have—I do.' I called his attention to the propriety of now making any additional requests that he might desire to leave. He repeated those he had made before, and added, 'I have put my house in order—I am ready to die '—and after a pause, 'where I die, there let me be buried.' Desiring to know what his views were, at this solemn moment, of our operations, I said, 'what do you now say of the work? Shall it go forward?' He immediately replied, 'what! the Mission? Yes,' with strong emphasis, 'let it go forward more than it ever has done.' His voice, naturally strong, had retained its force till now, in a remarkable degree; but getting perceptibly weaker, he became disinclined to more effort in speaking or moving than was necessary. He was evidently in close communion with God, on eternal things. On one occasion, he was heard to say, within himself, 'Away now with all worldly thoughts, all vain words;' and audibly prayed for his 'mother, brothers, and sister, and her children, that they might be given to God and His Church.' Sunday night was one of great restlessness and trial to himself and attendants. His symptoms had reached their highest degree of aggravation, setting at defiance all remedies, requiring constant motion and attendance, and portending rapid dissolution. He had generally been free from pain, and expressed his gratitude for so great a favor; but in the present stage he seemed to suffer greatly. When asked if it were so, his reply would be, 'not much,' or 'not now.' Throughout this last attack he had made a remarkable exhibition of the patience of the Gospel.

"On Monday morning it was evident that our dear brother was about to enter upon the scenes of eternity; there was a gradual increase in the severity of his symptoms, and all that could be done was to attend, alleviate, and wait for his death. About the middle of the afternoon, when a prominent symptom was at its height, and threatened immediate extinction to the remaining spark of life, he turned towards me and said, with an expression that cannot be described, 'Oh, Doctor, is there no relief for this?' Not in my power,' I replied, 'and such is its nature, dear brother, you cannot

long survive—you are now wholly in the hands of God.'
Turning his head again, he silently and meekly laid it
down, as it were, to die. Death was upon him. I now
asked if Christ was still as near and precious as he had
so often found him to be. 'Oh, yes, if I know my own
heart,' was his answer. Then, after a pause, he said
with fervor, 'Jesus, my master, *is near*—he is *very
near—now he is especially gracious.*' A few moments
of silence ensued, he then added, 'oh, I am *dying,*' trying, as it seemed, to realize the awful fact in all its mo-
mentuousness. 'Tell mother that my Saviour is now very
near—tell Mary'—here I mistook the precise exercise
of his mind, and requested an attendant to call Mrs.
Minor, who had left him for a moment. But he immediately added, 'No, don't call her—tell her *now*'—seem-
ing to know that the trying moment for her had not
arrived, though it was evidently at hand.

" He continued two or three hours after this, and
in prayer, as much as his symptoms would permit,
calmly awaiting his summons into the presence of his
God. During this period, I twice raised him up at his
request, the better to meet his symptoms. Each time,
he fainted, when I verily thought his spirit had taken
its flight. The last time he was evidently expiring,
and I held him in my arms, momentarily expecting he
would be a corpse. He revived, however, just enough
to say, 'lay me down.' As I did so, he turned over
on his left side unassisted, and after a few moments,
said audibly, distinctly, and with unceasing energy as
he spoke, 'I am dying—farewell mother—farewell sister
—farewell brethren of the ministry.' He then bade

farewell to his wife, and added, ' farewell brethren, I
have never regretted coming to Africa—farewell all.'
After a short pause, he added, ' let all payments be
liberally made, and my boy John, see that he be
well rewarded for what he has done for me.' He
then ceased to speak, and, in a few moments more,
breathed forth his spirit into the hands of Him who
gave it. So calmly and silently did he expire, and so
little changed in death, that I was at a loss for a time,
to know whether he had indeed departed."

" Thus died our first fallen Missionary! He had
' fought a good fight,' and had ' finished his course with
joy.' ' Tell my mother,' he said, ' that I die not' only
willingly, but joyfully.' Among his last expressions
were the touching words of his Saviour, when like him
commending a beloved relative to the care of a faithful
friend. Looking upon his wife, who stood near his bed,
he turned his eyes upon Mr. Payne, and said, ' Behold
thy sister.'

> Thou art gone home! from that divine repose
>   Never to roam!
> Never to say farewell, to weep in vain,
> To read of change in eyes beloved, again—
>   Thou art gone home!
> By the bright waters now thy lot is cast,
> Joy for thee, dear brother! thy bark hath past
>   The rough sea's foam!
> Now the yearnings of thy soul are still'd,—
> Home, home! thy peace is won, thy heart is fill'd,
>   Thou art gone home!"

CHAPTER XXIV.

Letter from the Rev. J. Peterkin, illustrative of Mr. Minor's character.

WE cannot better sum up the character of this devoted servant of God, than in the words of an intimate friend and brother in the ministry, the Rev. J. Peterkin.

"My acquaintance with Brother Minor commenced at the Theological Seminary of Virginia, he being in the class before me, as well as my senior in age. We were, however, a whole year together in that institution, without having formed anything like an intimacy. Not long after my entrance into the seminary, he requested my assistance in his Sunday school, at Fall Church, but as I found employment nearer home, and felt unable to take so long a walk, about seven miles, I declined joining him. This refusal, I am sure Brother Minor did not like, as he had very little to say to me during the remainder of the session. The truth is, he had made several similar applications in vain, and being able and willing to undergo so many privations himself, he probably did not make much allowance for the inability or unwillingness of weaker brethren. With all this, he was kind and considerate, but he seemed to regard it a solemn duty, both by precept and example, to urge those around him to works of faith and labors of love.

" Early in 1836, as he was then particularly in need of aid, I consented to accompany him to the school above mentioned, and immediately we were on the most intimate terms. Many an hour did he beguile, as we walked together by the way, in referring, either to his past life or his future plans. His heart was full of Africa, and in one of his earliest conversations with me, he expressed his determination to be a missionary there, but that a mother, aged and blind, and whom he tenderly loved, would regard such a step as an immediate and final separation. He himself, did not suppose that he could survive many years in Western Africa, and hence, at one time, he thought of Abyssinia as a field of labor, and at another time, of China. But all this was in deference to the opinion of his friends. It was his own conviction that it would be better to go to Western Africa, and labor for a short period, than elsewhere, with the probability of a more protracted life. My own belief is, that he would not have lived long anywhere, for though he did not despise life, he despised danger; and had he escaped a violent death, his impaired constitution could not have held out under the fatiguing labors to which, in any situation, he would have been subjected.

" He has been known to plunge into a river without hesitation, when some difficulty occurred about his being ferried over, and this was precisely characteristic of the man ; once let the course of duty be settled, and forward would he go, without anxiety as to the consequences. He possessed, as you are aware, great powers
9*

of endurance, but these, I think, were in a good **degree,**
the result of cultivation, rather than the product of nature. If on any occasion, when he had walked seven
miles to his Sunday school, and had declined stopping
with a friend to take dinner on his return, anything occurred to call him away at tea-time, he seemed never to
remember that his fast, since morning, remained unbroken.   *   *   *   *   *   *   *   *   *   *   *   *
Whatever he did, he seemed to think that another, possessing a willing heart, could also do; thus he has insisted on it, when I have complained of fatigue, that if I
would but exert myself properly, I might soon walk thirty
miles a day and preach three times; and this he himself,
when in health, would have considered no hardship. I
need hardly tell you that Minor was of an eminently
generous disposition. Anything approaching to parsi-
mony was his aversion, and yet I have known of his
walking from Washington to Alexandria to save twelve-
and-a-half cents, steamboat fare, when that sum was
important to him for the purchase of tracts. In fact, he
had an eye to everything, however small, that might
be used for the promotion of his Master's cause. I shall
always remember the large round box, intended mainly
for pennies, and marked ' China Mission,' but afterwards
altered, I think, to 'Africa,' which, during his stay at
the Seminary, hung by the hall door of the south building. It was a trifling matter to collect pennies, but, if I
mistake not, the amount raised at the Seminary for missions, during the period referred to, was unusually large.
So also at the Sunday school of Falls Church, that the
scholars should contribute to missions, was as well un-

derstood as that they should recite their lessons, and everything was done, by precept and example, to interest them in the good cause. I may here remark, by the way, that so great was Brother Minor's usefulness and influence at the place just referred to, that he was earnestly importuned, by many of his acquaintances, to make it his permanent field of labor ; but, as he declared to a kind friend in the neighborhood, Mr. Dulany, whose hospitality both Minor and myself often experienced, he felt called of God to go to Africa. The path of duty seemed plain—a divine impulse urged him on, and hence, in his farewell address, he could, with truth, declare to a sorrowing congregation,

> ' I see a hand you cannot see,
> Which beckons me away ;
> I hear a voice you cannot hear,
> Which bids me not to stay.'

" In two particulars, I think that Minor's character has been greatly misunderstood. He has been regarded as of an unsocial disposition, and, in temperament, approaching to the stoic. The mere fact, that he was habitually under the influence of a grand master-passion, will sufficiently account for these opinions. He was distant and reserved, at times, because his soul was absorbed in the contemplation of a subject, in which those with whom he held intercourse were not always interested. At that subject he had been looking so long and so intensely, that he could not, on every trifling occasion, turn his thoughts another way. It was only when his darling theme was made the topic of conversation that he appeared to real advantage ; then the countenance became animated, and the eye was at once radiant with the concealed fire of the soul.

"Minor was no stoic. He felt pain like other men, and acknowledged it, though he did not often complain. His heart, which many thought cold, was, in reality, awake to the tenderest susceptibilities of our nature ; but those who looked at him only, as it were, upon the surface, were little aware of the deep and strong emotions which struggled within. For the members of his own immediate family, including his brothers, from whom he had been long separated, he ever cherished the warmest affection, and would, I am sure, have devoted his life to the promotion of their individual happiness, had he not felt called to the higher work of promoting the happiness of mankind. His love for Virginia, the land of his fathers, was ardent and sincere ; and the very man, who was thought to have no local attachments, and to prefer the life of a wanderer, has sat down under the trees which sheltered him in childhood, and wept like an infant when about to bid adieu to their shade. He left them, not that he loved his country less, but that he loved God more.

"I have, thus far, said not a word of Mr. Minor's acquirements, nor am I sure that a notice of them is expected in this hasty sketch. It may not, however, be amiss to remark that his attainments in almost every branch of science were considerable. His compositions wanted finish, but whatever he said or wrote was to the point, and consequently, he seldom said or wrote any thing in vain. Dr. Keith, I know, regarded him as

a good theologian, sound, but not showy. With a view
to the missionary work, he had acquired some knowledge of medicine, and in botany and geology he was
perfectly at home. I remember once to have heard an
intelligent gentleman, whom he had met as a stranger
in travelling, express great admiration of his acquirements in this last department of science, and great surprise too, that a man who had so keen a relish for
scientific pursuits, should devote himself to the life of a
missionary. No man, I imagine, could more fully adopt
the words of the poet :

> 'There's nothing bright above, below,
> From flowers that bloom to stars that glow,
> But in its light, my soul can see
> Some token of the Deity.'

" Of a naturally inquiring mind, he sought an acquaintance alike with the works of nature and of art,
and wished to know the *why* and *wherefore* of every
thing. On one occasion, I heard some of the students
laugh at him because they had gone together to witness
a launch, and his curiosity had led him to get on board
the vessel, he was carried to the opposite side of the
river, and subjected to a long walk in order to return.
' Yes,' said he, ' you saved that trouble, but you came
away no wiser than you went; whereas, in case of
need, I could now launch a vessel.'

" I have mentioned that the productions of his pen
wanted finish, but they were, notwithstanding, full of
interest from their simplicity. In public speaking, there
was evidently no effort to overwhelm or astonish, or
even to please, yet this last effect was generally pro-

duced. He was a great admirer of pure Saxon, and
some of his missionary sermons, which were in conver-
sational tone and in Bible style, were in the highest degree interesting.

"After listening to one such, not long before his last
return to Africa, I remarked, 'Brother Minor, you read
the Bible a great deal.' 'I am only surprised at myself,'
replied he, ' that I read any other book.' My whole intercourse with Minor served to confirm me in an opinion
which I have long entertained, namely, that the cultivation of an enlarged missionary spirit will do more than
any thing else towards supplying the wants of home.
My own impression is, that before he left this country,
Minor did more, as a lay-reader and Sunday school
teacher, than some ministers accomplish in their whole
lives. His regard for those around him was not the less
ardent because he wished to do good to such as were
afar off. I have known more than one individual reclaimed
from habits of the grossest intemperance through his in-
strumentality, and this, not so much by means visible to
the public eye, as by private visiting and earnest prayer.
An aged, grey-haired man, a professor of religion, once
told me that he considered Brother Minor his spiritual
father; and I am very sure that many of his Sunday
scholars (some of whom it is believed became hopefully
pious,) regarded him in the same light. I may mention
too, that this same man, whose bones now rest beyond
the Atlantic, and whose soul was so large as to com-
pass the world in its aspirations, negligent as he might
be, of his own personal concerns, was the very man
who, on a stormy day, would remember to trudge

through rain or snow to carry a morsel of bread to some
destitute neighbor. If Robin, an aged and infirm African yet lives, he can testify how often, when his little
hut was blocked up with snow, the tall thin form of our
deceased brother would stoop to enter, bearing the welcome fragments from the Seminary table. In this case,
most unquestionably, when the eye of the missionary
looked abroad, it did not overlook home; when his heart
melted in tenderness over the miseries of the heathen,
it was not, it could not be indifferent to the woes which
were nigh at hand. Who joined, I might ask, with
hearty zeal, in every plan for the diffusion of education,
by day-schools, throughout the neighborhood? Minor!
Who was, by way of eminence, the laborious and
untiring Sunday school teacher? Minor! Who was
one of the most consistent and persevering advocates
of the temperance reform, in a vicinity where the
benefits of that reform could not but be seen and acknowledged? Minor! One might have supposed these
small matters to be beneath the notice of a man whose
bosom swelled with designs so great; but they were not.
Like his Divine Master, he 'went about doing good,'
and seized every occasion to advance the temporal and
spiritual welfare of his fellow men."

In compliance with his request, Mr. Minor was
buried at Cavalla. Upon the stone which covers his
mortal remains are inscribed his last memorable words:
"Let the Mission go forward; let it go forward more
than ever." Thus did the faith which never faltered in
life, grow yet stronger as the shadows of death gathered

around him. His work was done, and as its toils, its
perils, and its sufferings passed in review before him,
there was no regret for the past, no *despondency for the
future*. Ah! may we not believe that as those last
words fell from his lips, some blessed vision of that future
was vouchsafed to the departing soul—some glimpses
of that day-spring of light and glory which was yet to
break upon that benighted land? "Let the Mission go
forward!" The dead speaketh. The voice comes from
the eternal world. Waft it, ye winds, that the stirring
call may be caught and answered by a myriad tongues.
"Let the Mission go forward," sustained by the prayers
and by the offerings of the Church, and with Omnipo-
tence itself pledged for its success; let it go forward, to
yet more glorious conquests over the powers of sin and
darkness.

CHAPTER XXV.

AFTER Mr. Minor's death, the care of his Station was intrusted to his faithful interpreter, Musu, who continued to discharge its duties with remarkable ability and diligence, until the appointment of another missionary. As this young man may be regarded as the first fruits of Mr. Minor's labors, we introduce here, the account of his conversion, related by himself.

" When Mr. Minor first come, I go hear gospel, and I say, what for this man leave his fine country to come here ? This country no good for white man ; he be sick, he die ; what for he come ? This word he speak, must be true. So I take off my greegree, and hang him up. People say, ' what for you do that thing ? Bye and bye, greegree make bad palaver for you.' But I let gregree hang three moons; no palaver catch me. Then I take greegree and hang him up in rain ; hard rain come, beat on greegree, and I say, ' greegree, s'pose you be such great thing you can take care me, you can take care yourself.' So I let him be in rain till he get rotten. Then I say, ' greegree no good. I no wear him more.' "

Soon after Mr. Minor's decease, a serious quarrel arose between two towns in the immediate vicinity of the Station, and Mr. Payne determined to visit the scene of conflict, with the hope of acting as mediator, and averting a threatened war between the conflicting parties. We quote the following passages from his journal, as affording a lively picture of the character and condition of the natives.

"Taking with me two aged Tehlaoh, or lawyers, from my own place, I proceeded to all the parties involved in the quarrel, from town to town, to ascertain the real state of things. And I must observe, by the way, that my opinion of African native talent has been greatly elevated while listening, as my knowledge of the language enabled me to do, to the speeches of my Grebo lawyers, Indeed, if a knowledge of the laws, customs, and usages of his people, and those with whom he has intercourse, the ability to apply this knowledge calmly, judiciously, and impartially, to settling matters of controversy, and the power of enforcing his reasonings by frequent, copious, and striking similes and illustrations, should entitle him to such a character, then I do not hesitate to pronounce Krah Leah, one of the men brought with me, the Grebo Tehlaâ, an able African statesman.

"Having gone through nearly the whole Plabo tribe, collecting information, and enlisting the influence of neutrals, we ascertained that the Nyimlepo would consent to no overtures for peace so long as their property was in the possession of their enemies. Accordingly, the first thing we did, was to demand of the Neapo, the

trade goods which they had taken from the prisoners.
After much talking and objecting, it was, at length,
agreed that the goods should be placed in the hands of
the arbitrators, to be retained by them until the matter
was finally adjusted. The obstacle having been thus
removed, we next summoned the Nyimlepo to meet
their adversaries, with the arbitrators, in the oldest
Plabo town, to discuss and settle the whole matter.
Many objections and fears were urged against doing so ;
but, at length, a reluctant assent was obtained to meet,
though they could not be induced to fix upon any time.

Mr. Payne now entertained hopes of being able to
bring the palaver to a peaceful termination, but the very
next day, a new outrage was committed by one of the
parties, and the affair assumed even a more threatening
aspect than before. Several prisoners had been seized,
and the ensuing scene is thus described : "As soon as
information of the capture of their people reached the
Neapo town, the air was rent with the wailings of
the mothers, the sisters, and the wives of the captured.
They ran through and around the town, throwing their
limbs and bodies into every variety of wild and violent
gesture. The town drum beat. All seized their cutlasses and guns. Then, bedaubing their faces with
black paint, sticking bunches of black, sooty feathers over
both ears, or on the top of their head, girding around
their loins monkey skins, and cartouch-boxes made of
leopard skins, with long straps of the same, dangling
down to the ground—the very personification of one's
youthful conceptions of devils, they sallied frcm the town
pell-mell, throwing their guns into the air and catching

them, ringing bells, blowing horns, brandishing cutlasses, and calling out, 'come on! come on! let us go
over—let us cross at once and fight!' Their adversaries
professed equal willingness to fight. Painting and dress-
ing themselves in a still more hideous manner, realizing
the worst conceptions of savage barbarity—for they are
a peculiarly savage people, being the same, who, while
Mr. Minor was here, plotted the capture of a Dutch
vessel lying off the river—they ran down the side of
the river to its mouth, within a stone's throw of Neapo,
shouting, dancing, ringing, singing, and calling out, 'yes,
come on! come on Kraplo, (the headman of the Neapo,)
you man with a crooked neck—you rich man clothed in
a ragged garment—you toothless man—you poor fellow,
who since your father's death, have never been able to
build you a house; you who have to work your own
farm, having no one to assist you. Yes, come on! let
us fight!'

"Fearing that the prisoners might be killed, after
dispatching a messenger to call the king of Grand Taboo,
who had been acting with me, in trying to settle the
controversy, I hastened across the river. To a stranger,
all hope of saving the prisoners would have appeared
foolish. 'Let us kill them!' 'Let us bring them and
cut them again.' 'I will kill one.' 'I will take off his
head.' Such language, accompanied with the most violent, fiendish gestures, shouts, dancing, and singing,
alone met the ear. The women too, were dancing and
joining in the savage triumph. 'My heart rejoices,'
said an old woman to me, as I entered the town. 'They
(the Neapo,) caught five of my children, and now we

have caught them.' Having got an interview with
Nima, the father of the town, he assured me that no
further injury should be done to the prisoners. It was
a sickening scene, indeed ; but it was some relief to learn
that, amidst all the show of rash and heedless rage, the
principle which governed the multitude was ' an eye for
an eye, a tooth for a tooth;' those having received most
injury amongst the prisoners, who had been most active
in torturing their own people, when in their power.
One man assured me that all obstacles to ' settling the
palaver' were now removed, their enemies having received, at their hands, the same treatment which they
had received from them."

"*Thursday, July* 13*th*.—This morning, the deputation from Grand Taboo, for which I sent yesterday,
called at the Mission House for me to accompany them
to the king's place, to demand the prisoners. I sent
them on, however, before, promising to follow myself,
as soon as I could get off. I then called Kraplo, the
headman of the Neapo, from whom the members of the
family at this station have always received great kindness, and after showing him that I had done all in my
power to avert the war, told him, that after demanding
the prisoners, if they were refused me, I should consider
my work done, and proceed home. He seemed convinced of the justness of my statement, and said, if I
wished, I could now leave the matter in the hands of
his own tribe.

"My parting with the son of Kraplo (Musu,) was
quite affecting. He seemed extremely reluctant to part
with me, urging me, by every consideration which he

could devise, to remain until the 'palaver' was fully settled. When, at last, he saw that I was determined to leave, he asked me with evidently deep emotion, what would become of him and the station in case war actually began? It seemed a great relief to him to learn that I should continue to visit him, as usual, until a teacher or missionary arrived. 'But,' continued he, 'when the missionary arrives, suppose he will not consent to settle where there is war; what then? I beg,' said he, 'Mr. Payne, if no teacher *will* come here, that you will send a canoe and take me and my wife away. *It is true,* I believe the Gospel and want to be led by it. Since this palaver began, my heart has never ceased to be troubled on account of it.' "

Mr. Payne returned to his station without having been able to accomplish his object, but the " palaver" was, soon afterwards, happily adjusted without further bloodshed. Upon receiving intelligence that the difficulty was at an end, he repeated his visit to Taboo, where he had an opportunity of witnessing the following singular ceremony. " A living sheep was brought ; one or two persons from each of the contending parties, with sticks, now commenced beating the sheep, and continued the operation until every bone in it was crushed, and ' the palaver was broken.' "

CHAPTER XXVI.

ABOUT this time, the A. B. C. F. M., having determined to remove their Mission to the Gaboon River, relinquished their two stations at Rocktown and Fishtown, the charge of which was conditionally assumed by our own missionaries. Native teachers were stationed at both, under the superintendence of the Rev. Mr. Hazlehurst.

In August, the Rev. Dr. Savage, accompanied by Mrs. Minor, arrived in the United States. The object of his visit was the restoration of his health, and the securing, if possible, an addition to their reduced number of laborers.

Hitherto, the Mission, although encompassed with those difficulties which are naturally attendant upon the work, had encountered no opposition, either political or religious, from the natives of the country. The preaching of the Gospel had been freely tolerated, the schools sustained, and the persons and property of the missionaries respected. But now, a threatening crisis arrived, the nature of which will be best explained by extracts from the Rev. Mr. Payne's Journal. As it forms so important a part of the history of the Mission, we may be pardoned for quoting largely from this record.

" *Sunday, November 12th*, 1843.—This morning, had scarcely any people at Church, in consequence of a palaver connected with my having exchanged notes with a British Captain, who anchored yesterday off this place. The circumstances of the case are these. The Captain, having learned yesterday from a Krooman, that a foreigner resided on shore, kindly sent me some English papers. I acknowledged the receipt of them and invited the Captain to spend the next day, being Sunday, with me on shore. He accepted my invitation, and was at my house to-day at twelve o'clock. It appears that when he began to trade yesterday, he paid a particular kind of goods, much valued by the natives, to induce them to trade freely ; he told them, however, at the same time, that on the next day, he could not give this kind of goods, but something inferior. Accordingly, when the people went off this morning, the Captain (for he must needs trade on Sunday !) offered an inferior article. Some mischievous spirits at once suggested that Payne's note had done the mischief. It was to no purpose that I had never interfered with their trade—that the price given by the Captain was less than they received on shore. It was too good an opportunity for the devil to let pass for stirring up strife, and accordingly, as soon as the Captain came on shore, the people began to persecute my interpreter, who had been guilty of the sin of sending off my note. He came, with three men who speak English, to ask me and the Captain if we had written anything about trade. We assured them we had not ; but this did not satisfy. They sought a palaver with poor G., and one they would make. They required of him to pay the value of one hundred dollars, a sum which scarcely any native could raise, or they would drive him from the country. The matter, however, was compromised by their taking, for G. steadfastly refused to pay anything for a lie, about the value of six dollars. A lie, however, as this is, the devil has made it the instrument of stirring up much strife and ill feeling amongst the people, and causing them to 'speak all manner of evil against us falsely.'

"*Monday, November* 13th.—Knowing how common a thing it is amongst this people to eat and devour one another's property without cause, particularly during the present season, when they have nothing else to do, I had hoped that the affair of the Captain would terminate with G. But not so. I was the offending party. I had money—why should not I be made to pay?—said the evil spirits of Cavalla. They, accordingly, went to work to force me to pay for their lie. And what course, thought they, would sooner bring me to terms than to break up my school? They determined to adopt this course. This morning, while we were sitting at breakfast, without having sent any message to me on the subject, or in any way intimating that there was any charge against me, a large party of men and boys, some armed with cutlasses, entered our yard and houses, and drove off every child and native, in whatever capacity, from our premises. We, however, offered no resistance, and finished our breakfast.

"*Tuesday, November* 14th.—This morning, learning that the old men, to whom I have always looked for protection in difficulties, were about to leave this place

10

to attend a grand council of the Grebo tribe, about to convene at Cape Palmas, I sent to town, by the hands of my assistant teacher, a communication enumerating my grievances, and asking for redress. I complained, 1st. That strangers had been forced from my premises, contrary to the custom of their own country, as well as to that of civilized ones. 2d. The female scholars, whose betrothment money had been paid by the Mission, in consideration of services to be rendered by youths to whom they were betrothed, and over whom, therefore, the people had no control. 3d. That all this had been done without ever having given me the slightest intimation of any crime alleged against me. I demanded, therefore, the immediate return of the girls or the money which had been expended on their account, and also payment for the outrage. At the same time, I stated that I was ready to go to town and talk the matter over with the people, as soon as the children should be returned to school.

"Through the influence of the old men, most of the girls were returned, but the people refused to allow the boys to come back, or to pay any thing until I should go to town and 'talk the palaver.' This I declined doing, until the punishment, which had been inflicted upon me without a hearing, should be withdrawn.

"*Wednesday, Nov. 15th.*—The people were not at all satisfied with the stand which I had taken in regard to their conduct. That one man should oppose himself to a multitude, though their cause might be confessedly wrong and his right, was something that these people could not understand. Still less could they comprehend

that he would not yield. They, therefore, determined
to adopt more extreme measures. To-night, about 8
o'clock, the Sedibo (literally, freemen,) ran out of town,
and in a tumultuous and threatening manner, approached
our house and published, for this body makes laws, the
following mandates: 1st. That none of our boys belonging to the Cavalla, should come into our yard. 2d.
That they should wear only such clothing as is worn by
children of their age amongst their people, (in most cases
none.) 3d. That no one, wearing clothes, should go to their
town, and that I should not go to the chapel to preach.
4th. That the people should not attend religious services. 5th. That the scholars, while in town, should
not attend worship at G.'s house, as had been the custom. 6th. That no one should be seen reading a
book.

" *Thursday, November* 16th.--This morning the
books which I had sent to town for the boys to read,
were brought home. I was informed, too, that the boys,
who thus far had associated together, had been forbidden
to do so; and that they had been compelled to lay aside
their Mission clothing for such as was given them by
their friends, and some of them were in a state of perfect nudity. My interpreter told me that at one time
they forbade his coming to my house, but that he told
them plainly he would come, and they desisted. I
suppose the prohibition to our going to town, if ever
made, was withdrawn, as nearly all our family have
passed through it to-day.

" It has been most gratifying to witness the manner in which our Christian boys, and, indeed, all our

scholars have received this persecution. As long as they
were permitted to do so, they remained together, and
whenever they dared, came secretly, at night, to see us.
We received from them three or four notes, expressing
their sympathy with us, and reminding us that we were
suffering the common lot of Christians, as well as that
of their Lord and Master, Jesus Christ. As many as
have been permitted by their parents to do so, have gone
to other stations connected with the Mission."

Three weeks passed without any favorable change in
the people, and the Sedibo having forbidden any one to
attend preaching, the Sabbath services were necessarily
suspended. Mr. Payne again writes :

" *Tuesday, December 5th.*—This afternoon the Sedibo came again to our house, and took forcibly away,
the second time, our girls, together with some boys
from other towns and tribes, who had come to us secretly. The cause of this new outrage was the following : For the last six weeks, the headmen of the Grebo
tribe have been assembled in general council at Cape
Palmas, as before stated, to settle their difficulties with
one another, and with the surrounding tribes. At the
close of their conference, they determined to raise the
price of their produce fifty per cent. They made known
their determination to the Governor, who refused to
give their price. They then passed laws, that all native
children, in whatever capacity they might be, should
be taken from the Americans; and that no intercourse
with them should be allowed, until their demands were
granted. Our school girls, they said, were included.
Their laws further declared, that nothing of any de-

scription should be sold to Americans, and all strangers
from other tribes also, were to be prohibited from selling,
either to us or the colony.

"On hearing of these laws, and that it was the design of the people to break up our school, Brother
Smith, who was providentially with me, and I went to
town, and called the people together, to know the truth
of what we had heard. We were informed that such laws
had been passed, and that the Cavalla people were
determined to execute them, so far as they were concerned. We then read to them the written agreements
into which they had entered three months ago, by which
they had bound themselves, that in case of any controversy arising between them and the colony, in regard
to trade, we were not to be molested, until it was settled, when we should give whatever prices they might
agree upon. They said it was true that they had made
such an agreement, but their doings were annulled by
the voice of their tribe. We told them that whatever
power their council might have over their own boys, it
could not authorize them to drive strangers from my
premises, and still less, to interfere with the girls, whose
betrothment money had been paid by the Mission ; and
warned them against any interference with them. They
maintained that they would take all from the school.
As I had told them, however, that I intended to visit
Mt. Vaughan the next day, and should leave my wife
alone, they promised nothing farther should be done until
my return. I left them, relying upon their promise, but
scarcely had I reached my house, before a tumultuous
mob again entered, and dragged away all our children

except two, who had run upstairs and hid themselves under the bed. Fearing worse consequences, however, as soon as the people had gone, we sent them also, weeping bitterly at parting with us, to town.

"Mr. Smith's school, at the River Cavalla station, was broken up yesterday, and rumor says, the one at Mt. Vaughan also."

CHAPTER XXVII.

Intervention of the United States Squadron—Affecting scene.

THE condition of the Mission was now seriously alarming. It is true that all the opposition of the natives was avowedly only designed to raise the price of their produce, but there was reason to fear that this was only a pretence, covering other and more important objects. The various towns of the Grebo tribe had been united by their grand council under one head, King Freeman, and were bound to unite in any war which he might propose. The natives had entirely separated themselves from the colonists, which was considered an infallible sign of warlike intentions, and had included the missionaries in the "palaver," notwithstanding their written promise to regard them as distinct parties. It was currently reported that the natives were on the eve of a war with the colony, and it was almost certain that, in case of hostilities, the missionaries would be also involved. Entirely defenceless and unprotected as was the little band at Cavalla, it was evidently their duty to remove to a place of greater security. But how was this to be accomplished? Mrs. Payne could not walk, and the natives would not carry her. It was

determined that Mr. Smith should proceed to Mt.
Vaughan, and, with Mr. Hazlehurst, request Commodore
Perry, then daily expected at Cape Palmas with the
United States squadron, to send down a vessel to take
them off. The journal continues:

" This afternoon, I received a note from Mr. Moore,
our teacher at Grahway, by the hands of a colonist, informing me that the squadron was in sight, off Cape
Palmas. We had little expectation, however, of seeing
anything of it to-day, not imagining how any message
could be sent to it, by our brethren at Mt. Vaughan, so
soon. We were not a little surprised, therefore, as we
stood upon our piazza, and were looking out, by a beautiful moonlight, upon the sea, to observe a large vessel
moving down majestically from the windward, and
presently come to anchor just off our house. At half-
past ten o'clock, just as we were retiring to bed, we
were startled by a loud rap at the front door. It was
opened, and four Kroomen entered, in man-of-war dress,
and delivered to me two letters, one from Mr. Hazlehurst, the other, from Captain Abbott, commanding the
United States ship Decatur. It appears that as soon
as Mr. Hazlehurst saw the squadron approaching, he
procured a canoe, and with two colonists,) no native
would accompany him,) went out to the flag ship Macedonian. Commodore Perry, immediately on getting information of our situation, made signals for the Decatur,
which had not yet come to anchor, to bear down the
coast, and for her commander to come on board his ship.
Captain Abbott received instructions to repair to this
place, and to render us any assistance we might need.

As soon as he came to anchor, he addressed to me the letter now received by the Kroomen, couched in the most kind, Christian terms, and offering to come on shore with an armed force, early in the morning, if necessary. In acknowledging his kind favor, I recommended him to bring the armed force ; as I had heard of threats to detain the Kroomen who brought his letter, and also, to seize his boats in case they were landed.

" *Thursday, December 7th.*—This morning, at nine o'clock, we saw four large boats, a smaller one, and a canoe, coming from the Decatur, towards the shore. In a short time, they had landed, and the Captain sent a Krooman to apprise me of the fact. I immediately proceeded to where he was, passing, on my way, through crowds of men, women, and children, who, with mingled feelings of dread, anxiety, and indignation, pressed forward to behold the new exhibition of Kubi Sedibo, (foreign soldiers) landing on their shores. Captain Abbott, who had brought out to me a letter of introduction from his pastor, the Rev. Mr. Hathaway, of Warren, Rhode Island, received me as a Christian friend, and we were escorted by a company of marines to my house.

" After breakfast, the Captain called together the head-men in our school house, to talk over our difficulties. He held in his hand the deed of the mission lot which the people had given us, together with their written agreement, lately made with us, not to involve the Mission in ' palavers' like that professedly existing between them and the Colonial authorities. He reminded them of our character and object in settling amongst them, and how necessary it was to accomplishing this

10*

object, that we should not be subjected to outrages like those which they had lately been committing upon us. If they were really friendly to us, let them, at once, restore our scholars and repair the injury which they had done to us. In conclusion, he informed them that he, and the squadron with which he was connected, had been sent by their great chief, not to make war, but to promote peace and good-will between Africans themselves, and between them and all Americans with whom they were connected. At the same time, if they injured Americans, they were at hand to protect them. This show of protection, I had hoped, would be sufficient to repress the lawless spirit at present abroad amongst this people, and settle our difficulties at once. I was disappointed. The head-men repeated the views which they had expressed to Mr. Smith and myself, and also their alleged grievances in the case of the British vessel. The Captain told them that they had abundant proof that the latter was a fabrication; and in regard to the former, their Council had no right to make them do wrong, and that they ought to fulfil their written agreement. In other words, they should return their children to school, and restore the money which they had made my interpreter pay, unjustly, for sending off my letter to the British vessel.

"Much loud and angry talk now ensued. Some said they must talk the matter over in town; others, that their General Council must meet; the greater part, that they could not retract the position they had taken. Perceiving that they would yield nothing, and that, therefore, our longer stay amongst them would be in vain, if it did not

place our lives in jeopardy, I requested Captain Abbott
to take us off, with such of our effects as we could remove at a short notice. We now commenced, with mournful hearts, to leave a place endeared to us by so many
trials and sufferings, toils and encouragements. As soon
as a boat load of things was got ready, Captain Abbott
embarked with them, leaving one of the lieutenants,
with other officers, to attend to the rest. When the
first baggage was put in the boats, there was much excitement, the people now realizing, for the first time,
that we were really about to leave. At this time, some
young men, who were attached to us, ran to our house
and entreated us not to leave. We continued our preparations. In the meantime, the people seemed to be
collecting from the surrounding small towns, with their
guns, apprehensive, as I suppose, of an attack from the
marines ; but no other demonstration of hostilities on
their part, that I am aware of, was made.

" At half-past two, P. M., we had packed up all our
things that we could conveniently take off, and were on
our way to the beach. Dr. Wolfley, of the Decatur,
was walking before me, with Mrs. Payne. Immediately
on passing through the gate, they were met by Yellow
Will, the second man in rank to Freeman in the Grebo
tribe, and the king of Cavalla. He entreated Mrs. Payne
not to leave, and the Doctor not to take her away. They
repeated the same request, with great earnestness, to
me. Yellow Will assured me that Freeman had called
the Grand Council to re-assemble, and that the ' palaver'
should be ' set' the next day, at Cape Palmas. I told
him, when I heard that everything was settled I might

think of returning.   The concourse of people assembled
on the beach as we passed along, exceeded anything I
had ever seen.   The whole population of Cavalla, about
four thousand souls, must have been present to witness
the strange spectacle before them.   A most touching
scene was presented just as we were embarking.   G.,
my interpreter, who has remained faithful to us in all
our difficulties, was taken ill about a week ago.   He
was much persecuted, even after he was taken sick, by
his heathen townsmen, who would taunt him, as they
passed by his house, with such expressions as these;
' He said he trusted in God, let us see what his God will
do for him ?'   ' He renounced the customs and greegrees of his fathers, and what has now befallen him ?'
Others would say, ' He is not sick, he only feigns to be,
to save himself from palavers, or to induce Payne to
send him good food.'   These expressions were so painful
to him, that two days ago he begged me not to visit him.
I continued, however, to do so, or send him medicine,
until yesterday, when my messenger returned to me
with the information that G. could not be found.   His
near relatives had hid him, as usual, in cases of severe
illness, for fear of witchcraft.   On hearing that I was
about to leave, however, he caused himself to be taken
back to his house, and sent a boy to inform me of it.   I
told the messenger that I would see him before I left ;
but so much had I to occupy my mind, that I had almost
forgotten my promise, when, to my astonishment, I was
told, about one o'clock, that he had been brought to the
house and desired to see me.   On going into the room
where he was lying, he fixed his sunken eyes upon me,

and thus addressed me, 'Mr. Payne, have I not always
told you that I wished to accompany you wherever you
go, and to die in the Mission? and now you are going
away to leave me to die among my enemies. I know
you are a God-man, (preacher of the Gospel) but I do
not think *I* could have treated *you* so.' I assured him
how sorry I had been at the thought of leaving him, but
had supposed that his state of health and the opposition
of his friends would prove insuperable obstacles to his
removal. Still, if it was his request, I would ask the
Captain to have him taken on board the ship. He said
it *was* his request. The Captain most cheerfully granted
it, and Dr. Wolfley, on learning the circumstances, took
a most lively interest in his case. He was placed in a
hammock, and taken to the place of embarkation. And
now came the mournful spectacle. Some of his most
intimate friends and nearest male relatives pressed around
him, and besought him, with tears, not to leave the
country. His women wept bitterly. Two female relatives, however, of his father's family, fixed the attention
of all spectators. The one, judging from her shrivelled
form and tottering step, and sunken cheeks, had passed
threescore years and ten ; the other was a middle-aged
woman. As the hammock was lying on the ground,
they threw themselves down, and rolling over in the
sand, cast their arms around in wild gesticulations, accompanied with the soul-rending wailing and cries
which only heathen can make. When the boat in which
G. was placed hauled off from the shore, they followed
it in water up to their necks, plunging into the raging
surf, and making all those passionate exhibitions of feel-

ing usual on accompanying a near relative to his final resting place. Indeed, they expected to see their relative no more, and there was too much reason to fear that their expectation was well founded. At three, P. M., we were all safely on board of the Decatur. The Captain gave us his stateroom, and made us as comfortable as sea sick people could possibly be."

CHAPTER XXVIII.

Commodore Perry's parley at Cape Palmas—The squadron visits Little Bereby—Overtures of natives to Mr. Payne—Fidelity of Mission scholars —Another deputation from Cavalla—The " palaver set."

On the following morning, the Decatur came to anchor off Cape Palmas, where lay also the Macedonian and Saratoga. The colony was in a state of great excitement and alarm, and in the course of the morning, the Commodore went on shore to meet the Governor and delegates from the various towns, with the hope of settling their difficulties. He explained the respective rights of the natives and colonists, and commended the character and design of Christian Missions. He enjoined upon the people the duty of living in peace, recommending that they should immediately restore their children to the schools, and remove Mr. Payne's effects to Cavalla, should he wish to return after they had made a proper apology for their past ill-treatment. Intimidated by the presence of a large armed force, they agreed to all the Commodore's proposals, and separated ; but it still remained doubtful how far their promises were worthy of credit. The squadron sailed the next day for Little Bereby, and there can be no doubt that the punishment there inflicted for the outrage commit-

ted some months before upon the captain and crew of
the Mary Carver, had great influence in preventing the
recurrence of hostilities at Cape Palmas.

Late in the afternoon of the same day, a delegation
came from the Cavalla people to Mr. Payne, who thus
writes :

" They had been sent, they said, by their people, to
apologise to me for the injury they had done me, with
the promise that they would carry my things back to
the station free of expense, and restore all my scholars
as soon as I would return to demand them. I replied,
that I had learned, by sad experience, to distrust all
their promises, and that if they really wished to treat
with me about returning to them, they must give some
more substantial proof of their penitence for the past, and
good intentions for the future, than mere words. In
short, that they must pay me four bullocks, for the outrage which they had committed against me. This demand was made with the concurrence of the other
members of the Mission, as the best means of preventing a repetition of the injury from which we now suffer.

" *December 20th.*—This afternoon ten men came
from Cavalla to bring me three bullocks, having brought
one a few days ago, thus completing the number required of them to ' set our palaver.' I had heard, however, from very good authority, that these bullocks were
taken from the family of my interpreter, as a fine upon
him for having taken off my letter to the trading vessel,
which, as before stated, was the innocent cause of our
difficulties ! I told the people that I could not, therefore, receive the bullocks, until I could send and ascer-

tain the truth of this report, since, if true, I could have nothing to do with them."

"*Friday, December 22d.*—Having ascertained, in a satisfactory manner, that the bullocks were taken from my interpreter's family, and that the people threatened, moreover, in case these were returned and they had to pay their own, they would expel that family from the community, I concluded to send back the bullocks this morning to the people, with the message that I wanted no more bullocks, but wished to remove my remaining things from the station."

"*Sunday, December 24th.*—I spent to-day at Mt. Vaughan, and Brothers Smith and Hazlehurst being too unwell to attend church, I officiated morning and evening. On the latter occasion, I addressed sixty Mission children, collected together from its various stations. It was extremely gratifying to meet so many, in view of their having been lately scattered abroad. I felt great cause for gratitude and encouragement, that such a number of my little flock should have followed me, and, indeed, that all present gave such satisfactory evidence of their attachment to the Mission, as was manifested by their assembling together at this time. In concluding my remarks, I addressed first the Christians, and, after alluding to our late trials, asked them if they were still resolved to persevere in their Christian course. They all gave a hearty response in the affirmative. I then spoke to the children collectively, reminded them of the late efforts of their people to break up the schools, and our unchanging purpose to impart to them the blessings of education and religion, and appealed to them to know if they were determined to coöperate with us, and if they were, to rise up. Instantly every child stood up ; in the great majority of cases, I doubt not, in obedience to the spontaneous impulses of their heart."

" *Thursday, January 4th*, 1844.—To-day, another deputation was sent to me from Cavalla, consisting of one of the old men, the head of the Sedibo, and some others. It appears, from their statement, that the person by whom I sent back the bullocks, made the impression upon the people that I was unwilling, under any circumstances, to return to them. They had been sent, they said, to beg me to reconsider the matter. I told them that I was willing to return to them as soon as they should manifest such a state of mind as would render it of any use to do so. That their fining my interpreter's family, on my account, to obtain bullocks to send me, showed that their feelings were still unkind towards me. But that if the Cavalla people were willing to pay the bullocks, I would return. This, the Mission insisted upon, as the only satisfactory evidence they could give of regret for maltreating me, and of their sincerity in begging me to return. They appeared to receive my remarks in good part, and departed.

" Cape Palmas, *January 11th*.—After remaining here for five weeks in a state of suspense as to what course we ought to take, there seems now a fair prospect of things being settled in such a satisfactory manner at Cavalla, as to justify our speedy return thither. I learned yesterday, from a man who has been friendly to us in all our difficulties there, that the people had become very uneasy lest they should lose me altogether, in con-

sequence of having learned that I had made a visit to
Rocktown and Fishtown, and that this induced them to
send the last deputation. When that deputation returned, there was no objection whatever made to paying, in the manner required. Two of the bullocks have
been collected, and the people are only waiting to get
two more, to bring them up and ' set the palaver.' A
great reaction, it is said, has taken place, and the Sedibo,
the movers of all our troubles, are everywhere de-
nounced among the people.

" Now that the excitement connected with our late
difficulties has passed away, and we are enabled to take
a calm and dispassionate view of the circumstances attending them, much reason is seen for hoping that it will
result in good to the cause in which we are engaged.
The providential arrival of the squadron, just at the moment when the natives appeared to be intent upon a
general outbreak, not only put an end to that, but will
prevent the recurrence of similar ones. The prompt assistance rendered my family in the hour of danger, must
leave the impression upon the natives that the missionaries may have protection when they choose to claim it,
and prevent those acts of violence, generally the work of
a few leading evil spirits, which make an appeal for such
protection necessary. The fact, too. that I refuse to return to a people who persecuted me, and put the Gospel
away from them, until they retract their conduct, and
give pledges that it shall not be repeated, will make the
natives careful to restrain the few, who would injure the
country so far as to deprive it of our services. That such
may be the happy result, and that God, in this case,

may 'make the wrath of man to praise Him,' and 'in all things to be glorified,' is my constant prayer."

Early in March, 1844, Mr Payne returned to Cavalla, and re-opened his schools. He had been, for two months, employed in missionary duty at Mt. Vaughan, during the absence of the Rev. Mr. Hazlehurst, who had visited Sierra Leone, in the hope of benefiting his health by the voyage, and of procuring assistant teachers from the English schools at that place. The first communications of both these gentlemen to the Committee, after they had resumed the labors of their respective stations, contain the cheering intelligence of several native converts added to the Church, from among their scholars In May, Mr. Payne again visited Taboo. He found the mission premises in good order, and the pupils, whose number had increased to twelve, afforded gratifying evidence of Musu's conscientious fidelity to the duties of his position. The steadfastness of this young disciple, under all the discouraging circumstances of his situation, cannot but be regarded as a wonderful triumph of Divine grace. Neither persuasion nor threats could induce him to abandon his post, but, for nearly two years, he continued to superintend the station, with no encouragement except an occasional visit from Mr. Payne. These interviews were eagerly improved, as opportunities of acquiring information on various questions of duty.

On the present occasion, he inquired, "If meat is brought on Sunday, which I have reason to think was killed on that day, ought I to receive it? Is it right to give food to the hungry on Sunday? Ought any presents to be received on that day? What is the meaning of Redeemer?"

Another young man, who had also been under Mr. Minor's instructions, and who still manifested a desire for improvement, asked, " Is it right to eat of things offered in sacrifice to idols?" Thus was the seed, sown by the lamented Minor, springing up to the honor and glory of God. He had not been permitted to witness the fruits of his labors, but none the less surely were those labors seen and rewarded by the great Lord of the harvest. "One soweth and another reapeth," but both unite in ascribing all the glory to Him who alone giveth the increase.

The year which had now elapsed had been, in some respects, one of severe trial ; yet had it been marked by many and great mercies. The little band, indeed, missed from their ranks one of its most devoted and useful members, but the departed one had gone rejoicing to his rest, and his last words had been those of encouragement and hope. None other had been summoned to follow him, and though continued illness had obliged Mr. Appleby to leave the field for a time, they were now daily looking for the return of Dr. Savage, with a new accession to their number. The cloud, which had gathered with such portentous blackness, had burst in blessings. The Mission seemed only the more firmly established by the events which had so seriously threatened its overthrow. The missionaries had been gratified by convincing proofs of the sincerity and steadfastness of the young converts, whose affectionate adherence had solaced them in the midst of their trials, and other wanderers had, from time to time, been gathered into the fold of Christ.

CHAPTER XXIX.

Death of Warra Hobah, alias Alexander V. Griswold.

WHILE some of these young disciples were witnessing a good confession, amid scenes of toil and strife in their own benighted land, another was bearing his testimony to the power of Divine grace, far away in the quiet sick chamber, where Christian friends gathered to soothe, with their kind offices, the last moments of the African stranger.

Warra Hobah had entered the Mission school at Mt. Vaughan several years before, and had made such good use of the privileges there enjoyed, that the missionaries determined to send him to the United States, to learn the art of printing. He was one of the fifteen native youths supported by the scholars and teachers of Grace Church Sunday School, Boston, and by their request, had received the name of Alexander V. Griswold.

He had accompanied Dr. Savage to Boston, and had been received into the printing-office of J. R. Marvin, Esq., where his conduct was so exemplary, and his improvement so rapid, as to excite high hopes of his future usefulness. He resided with Dr. Perkins, who was, at the time, pursuing the study of medicine, with the intention of returning as a missionary physician.

On the 31st of October, Griswold addressed the following letter to his heathen father, the aged king of the Baboes : "I have very good friends here. I am living with Mr. Perkins. I am now learning to print, so as to come home and print books for our countrymen. I have seen the mighty works of the Lord. I have seen water, hard as stone and burns like fire. Witch never touch me. I am well. The Lord is with me; so you and all the old men ought to throw away your greegrees and serve God, because He, only, is able to save your souls from eternal punishment of hell. The leaves of the trees are falling off now, and as these leaves are falling, so we shall all fall. Oh! what a great punishment it must be to them that hear the word of God and do not do it ; if we do not love God for all the things he has done for us, and above all, for sending His only begotten Son, Jesus Christ, to die for us !"

He had passed through the severe winter of 1843–4 without injury to his health, but on the 5th of May, he was seized with a severe attack of inflammation on the lungs, a disease to which his countrymen seem particularly liable. Dr. Hale was immediately summoned, but notwithstanding all his medical skill, and the kind and faithful attentions of Dr. and Mrs. Perkins, the disease continued to make rapid progress, and on the night of the 16th, he breathed his last. The following letter from Dr. Perkins affords gratifying evidence of his preparation for death.

"During his sickness, Griswold has given us, I think,

good evidence that he was not unprepared to die.   In
the early part of his sickness, he told me he thought he
should not get well, but die.   I asked him if he was
willing to die.   'Yes, I am not afraid to die.'   Said I,
have not you been a great sinner; and you know God
hates sin, how can you go to heaven?   'I trust God has
forgiven me all my sins, and wiped them all out of his
book for Jesus' sake.'   If God should say you might
live or die, what would you do?   'I would say, just as
he chooses, God's will be done.'   What word do you
wish me to send to Dr. Savage, and to the school-boys?
'Ask Doctor to forgive me all bad things, and pray for
me.   Ask the boys to pray for me that I may return to
Africa, a printer, and print the Bible for my poor countrymen.'   Your father would say you were witched
now, would he not?   'Yes.'   But what do you say
about your sickness, are you witched?   'Tell my father
that witch is all foolishness; tell him God gave me to
you, and God has taken me away—bless his name.'   I
asked him if he would like to have prayers in the church
for him on Sunday.   He answered very quickly, 'Yes,
sir,'and then seemed to consider again what I had asked,
and repeated, 'Yes, sir, yes sir, very much indeed.'   I
then asked him what he thought the Lord intended by
sending this sickness upon him.   'To try me,' was the
reply.   He asked me, in a number of instances, to read
particular passages of Scripture, and would tell me
where I might find them.   He asked to have the twenty-
third chapter of Matthew read—at another time to have
the chapter about those who are blessed, which he said
was the fifth of Matthew—at another, the eighth of Ro-

mans, on the love of God. After reading this chapter, I reminded him of what he had said, ' that he should not recover,' and said, ' Griswold, perhaps God, who withholds no good thing from us, may see best for you never to return again to your country. He may see that if you should go back to Africa you would dishonor him, by again becoming a heathen ;' when he replied with great feeling, apparently of horror at the idea, ' God forbid !' "

" On Thursday he appeared near his end, and often prayed aloud in a firm and clear tone—' Oh, Lord ! forgive me all my sins for Jesus' sake.' I again asked if he was willing to die. He said, ' I ask not to live, I ask not to die ; if it please God to take me I am ready to go, I am not afraid to die.' Said I, ' is God with you now ?' Yes, he is always with me. Tell the school-boys that I am an example to them that they too must die, and stand before God in judgment.' ' What shall I tell your father ?' ' Tell him, praise the Lord, oh my father ; honor and worship him always, cast away all your greegrees and worship him alone.' About two hours before he breathed his last, he made a great effort to collect his thoughts, and prayed in such a tone and with such earnestness as I never heard before. The burden of his prayer was ' his poor country people and himself, and the love of Christ in saving us from the fire that never can be quenched.' When just ready to depart, he was asked, ' what would you do without Jesus ?' He said, ' I should be a miserable creature—I should be lost.' These were his last words."

Why was this interesting youth brought in safety
11

over the great waters, to sicken and die in a strange land? Man's wisdom could not fathom the reasons for a decree thus suddenly cutting off the promise of so much usefulness, but the humble Christian doubted not that the great Head of the Church knew best how to promote the interests of his own cause. Griswold's sojourn among us had been short, but many had rejoiced in the light of his Christian character, and glorified God on his behalf. The heathen boy, degraded almost to a level with the brute, transformed into the intelligent, enlightened, consistent disciple of Christ, had brought under the personal observation of many friends of the Mission convincing proof that its labors were not in vain, and strengthened their confidence in its future success. Those who acknowledged the worth of an immortal soul to exceed all the treasures of worldly wealth, felt, that had no other good been effected, the Church was more than repaid for all that had been expended or endured.

CHAPTER XXX.

Embarcation of another band of Missionaries—Cape Verde—Bathurst—
Sierra Leone—Monrovia—Arrival at Cape Palmas—Sickness—Chapel at
Cavalla—Examination of School.

On the 26th of May, 1844, another band of missionaries
set sail for the coast of Africa. Dr. Savage's appeal for
aid had not been in vain; and he now returned to his
work with a larger number than had ever before embarked at one time. His associates were the Rev. E.
W. Hening and wife, Mrs. C. L. Patch, and Miss Rutherford. Their voyage across the Atlantic was short and
prosperous, and on the first of July they welcomed their
first view of the African shore. The vessel was, however, for several weeks engaged in trade along the coast,
but the detention could hardly be regretted, as it gave
the new comers an opportunity of learning much that
was interesting and useful, in regard to the operations
of the other Missions, established at the different points
at which they touched. It will be interesting to follow
them in these observations, in extracts from the journal
of one of their number, who now rests from her labors.
Mrs. Patch addressed this journal, in an epistolary
form, to a sister at home.

"*July 1st—Cape Verde.*—I assure you the sight
of land is pleasant, be it ever so barren. The Cape ap-

pears inaccessible; the surf dashes against the rocks, which seem perpendicular and look very white in the bright sunlight. Very little vegetation is to be seen. You know that Cape Verde is the western extremity of Africa, that land of which I have heard so much, of its bondage, superstition and degradation.

"*July 2d—Goree.*—This is a French settlement, with a strong fortification. To-day passed Magdalen, Pierced and Bird Islands—saw one solitary tree. Pierced Island is so called from there being a large hole in the rocks, which might be taken for a work of art instead of nature.

"*July 4th.—Off Bathurst, River Gambia* —The vessel anchored here yesterday—this morning the gentlemen have gone on shore. Bathurst is an English settlement; there are about fifty Europeans, merchants and officers in the army, besides others, filling offices of trust, appointed by government. This afternoon, Rev. Messrs. Godman and Linn, Wesleyan Missionaries, called on us, and invited us to spend the day with them to-morrow. Dr. Savage and Mr. Hening brought us fruit and flowers; and indeed L. I am delighted to see something from land again. Oh, I have so much to be thankful for, I can but wonder and adore the goodness of my God!

"*July 6th.*—Passed the day, yesterday, at the Mission house, and visited the day school, where there were about one hundred children present; some of them read in the Testament very well, answered questions, and all sang very prettily. I was particularly pleased with the buildings; both school house and the chapel are large and airy. Bathurst is said to be unhealthy. Many wives of merchants have died here. How many are willing to sacrifice life, and to leave friends and country to make money, but if it is for the sake of teaching the Gospel, they are said to be beside themselves.

"*July 19th.—Off Sierra Leone.* The view from the vessel is most lively. The houses are embosomed in palm-trees and an endless variety of shrubs, vines and flowers. Freetown is situated at the foot of the mountains, and appears to be a busy place. It is the rainy season here now, and every thing is very damp. The mountains look beautifully green, and vegetation is very luxuriant.

"*July 24th.*—Yesterday, Rev. Mr. Dove met our party at the landing early in the morning, and escorted us out to Fourah Bay station. This is the High School of the Church Missionary Society, where boys are educated. Fourah Bay is about three miles from Free town, and one of the most lovely spots I ever beheld. The buildings are old, but the beautiful views around more than make up for this. I am told that there are many delightful, retired walks. The roads are perfectly smooth, and lined, on either side, with a variety of trees, shrubs and vines. The air was filled with odors from sweet flowers, from the pure white, to the bright red and yellow. There were twenty-nine boys present, many of them fine-looking. I never heard better singing ; music is one of their studies, and is thoroughly taught. The missionary at this station is the Reverend Mr. Jones, a colored gentleman. He is now on a visit to England, and Rev. Mr. Crowther has charge. When I reflect that all these boys are recaptured slaves, I rejoice that God has devised means for their rescue and for their education; some of them, I trust, may become preachers of the Gospel. Returned with Mr. Dove to breakfast, their usual hour being nine o'clock; rather later than New England people would fancy. I passed a pleasant day; saw many natives who came to sell mats, fowls, &c.

"*July* 27*th.*—I feel much indebted to Mr. Dove for his kindness. Yesterday morning, he met us again at the landing, and conveyed us to the Rev. Mr. Schön's, where we were to pass the day. Mr. S. is a missionary of the Church of England.

"*July* 30*th.*—I have made my last visit on shore. We left the vessel early yesterday morning, and crossed the river to pass the day with the Rev. Messrs. Badger and Amos. This station is the High-school of the Wesleyans; only Christian boys are admitted, and these are educated for the ministry. The buildings are very spacious and beautifully situated. The view of the mountains from the verandah is lovely and imposing. I was highly gratified with the exercises in school, and with the devout and quiet appearance which seemed to pervade the whole establishment.

"*August* 12*th.*—Cape Mesurado is a wild looking spot. Upon the summit of the promontory is situated the town of Monrovia. I liked the appearance of the people. It seemed natural- to be once more among Americans. Although many of them are very poor, they seem to be happy. They are free; true, there are those who do not work, and who would rather have a master to provide for them.

"*August* 17th.—I think it was about half-past three o'clock when we landed on Cape Palmas rocks. If I ever felt grateful in my life, it was then, when I found myself safely on land. Governor Russworm kindly provided us with a donkey and one vehicle, which enabled us, by riding in turn, to reach Mt. Vaughan a little after dark. Mrs. Thomson, with her twelve girls, met us at the top of the hill ; the tea-table was laid, and I really felt at home. The sickness of the Rev. Mr. Hazlehurst, and the feeble health of Mr. Smith, saddened me, as they must soon leave for America, and our band of laborers will be again reduced."

Mr. Hazlehurst had, at this time, just passed through a very severe and dangerous illness, which had so reduced him as to leave little hope of his recovery, except from the invigorating breezes of the ocean. The Rev. Mr. Smith's health had been greatly impaired by five years residence in Africa, and imperatively required a change of climate ; so that both these gentlemen were obliged to return to America in the same vessel which had brought the new comers. Dr. Savage took charge of the station at Mt. Vaughan, and here the strangers were comfortably accommodated while passing through their acclimation.

On the 3d of October, Mrs. Patch writes, " Five months, to-day, since I left Lowell. I have experienced many mercies ; the watchful care of my heavenly Father has been ever over me ; he has raised me up from the bed of sickness, and preserved me from 'the noisome pestilence.' Mr. and Mrs. Hening have recovered from the fever ; they were both quite sick—indeed, for a few

days, very ill. Miss Rutherford has had a slight intermittent—not confined to her room. I was in my room
about four days, so that it is not probable either of us
will have *the* fever."

All were now ready to engage in the active duties
of the Mission and anxious to begin their work. It was
decided that Mrs. Patch should become Mrs. Payne's
assistant at Cavalla, and on the 29th she removed to
that station. She records her first attendance at the
religious services held for the natives.

" *October* 31*st*.—Last evening I attended the weekly
lecture in town. The chapel is made of bamboo, with
a thatched roof, dirt floor, plain board seats, and desk
and table of the same; no glass in the windows, but
common board shutters. The lamp on the table is a
tin cup, filled with palm oil; a stick with a rag wrapped
around it answers as a substitute for tube and wick.
The service is in Grebo."

Mrs. Patch did not commence her regular duties in
the school until after the Christmas examinations, of
which we find the following notice.

" *December* 28*th*.—On the 24th was the annual examination. There were eighty-six pupils present, including the boys from three out-stations, besides Taboo;
and Tom Wilson's night school from town. I was highly
gratified by all the exercises. Some of the boys at this
station are considerably advanced in arithmetic and
geography, and write pretty good compositions."

CHAPTER XXXI.

IN the meantime, deputations from Fishtown, Rocktown and Taboo had visited Mt. Vaughan to see "the new God-man," and beg that either he or Dr. Savage would settle among their townsmen. After visiting all these places and carefully comparing their claims, Mr. Hening determined to devote himself in carrying on the work, so successfully begun by the lamented Minor at Taboo. Dr. Savage resolved to locate himself at Fishtown, and having been united in marriage with Miss Elizabeth Rutherford, removed thither in December, 1844.

Until the necessary arrangements for occupying these stations could be completed, Mr. and Mrs. Hening remained at Mt. Vaughan, where the native school was still in operation, and regular services were held in the chapel on the Sabbath; but the most of the scholars having been transferred to Fishtown, they now prepared to remove to their own station. Before their departure, they had the happiness of welcoming at Mt. Vaughan, Dr. and Mrs. Perkins and Mr. and Mrs. Appleby. Dr. Perkins had spent three years in Boston, pursuing the
11*

study of medicine, and Mr. Appleby had acquired a knowledge of the art of printing ; so that both returned prepared for increased usefulness in the service of the Mission.

Mr. and Mrs. Hening left Mt. Vaughan about the middle of February, arriving at Cavalla the same day. Here they found the people in a state of great excitement; a serious quarrel having arisen between two portions of the Grebo tribe, which threatened to provoke a general war. The dispute had commenced between the people of two towns, about some forest land which both were desirous of clearing for their rice farms. Other towns had soon taken part in the quarrel, and severe skirmishes had occurred, in which lives had been lost on both sides. Mr. Payne, having in vain endeavored to act as mediator, addressed a note to Governor Russworm, soliciting his interference between the contending parties. The Governor arrived at Cavalla on the 19th of January, and in conjunction with the native King of Cape Palmas, succeeded in obtaining a promise that "the palaver should be set." The ceremonies on this important occasion are thus described by Mr. Payne:

" *Monday, January* 20.——Early this morning messengers were despatched to Grahway and Wotteh, to procure a man from each of those places to go through the usual ceremony of 'setting the palaver.' About 11 o'clock, I was called by the Governor to witness the ceremony. I found on reaching the King's house, in the middle of the circle formed by the Governor and other arbitrators, together with the headmen of Cavalla, a wooden bowl, containing some water, and near by it, lying on the ground, some powdered preparation, which I was informed was *the liver of some man* who had been killed in war, burned with some vegetable matter. The three young men appointed to ·perform the ceremony in behalf of their people, now approached the bowl, dipped up water in their fingers three times, carried it to their mouths, and as often spit it out. Afterwards each dipped his fingers in the *powdered liver* four times, putting a portion each time in his mouth. Finally all the arbitrators, as well as other natives present, collected around the bowl, ate the remainder of the *liver* and then hastily dispersed."

There was much reason, however, to fear that this professed settlement of the difficulties was not entirely sincere. Mr. Payne had believed that, in the commencement of hostilities, the Cavalla people had not intended to destroy life, but the disposition of their opponents was evidently for war, and they had committed such unprovoked and unprecedented outrages, as it was hardly probable would be so easily forgiven by a savage and heathen people. It was soon apparent that hostilities would be renewed when both parties had completed their preparations for war. Occasional extracts from the journal of Mr. Payne will show the progress of the affair, and furnish additional illustrations of heathen customs.

" *Sunday, January 26th.*—On our way to church this morning, we passed an immense crowd of people, collected about a great ' war-man,' as he is called. I find, on inquiry, that this is the same individual who was here about three months ago, and made a ' greegree,' which he told the people would, on a certain day, insure them any quantity of fish they needed. His gree-gree having failed two or three days in succession, he suddenly left, as I thought, in disgrace. It would seem, however, that this was a mistake; for on the first rumor of war with Grahway, this same character makes his appearance, has a house erected for him by the people, and undertakes to prepare war 'greegrees,' which will make the balls of their enemies rebound from their bodies and fall powerless before them ! It was this ceremony which was attracting the crowd of people we now saw; and I was gravely told, that after having been rubbed over with the doctor's preparation, two men were shot at this morning, and saw the balls fall powerless before them in a bowl prepared to receive them ! Absurd as is such a pretension, it is, I believe, generally credited by the people, and proved sufficient to keep nearly the whole population from church. Only about five or six men were present, and in all, the attendance did not exceed seventy people.

"*Saturday, February 8th.*—This morning, our attention was attracted by an immense concourse of women, on the green in front of our house. It was a meeting of the Cavalla *women*, called by one of their number, to ascertain their feelings in regard to the proposed war ! Before taking the vote, they were arranged in two parties, one composed of the natives of Cavalla and neutral towns and tribes; the other, of those born in the towns upon which it is proposed to make war. This arrangement, however, having displeased the headmen, the meeting was broken up, without having accomplished its object. At four o'clock this afternoon, however, it was again convened ; and along with the women, nearly the whole Cavalla population assembled. An aged woman arose and narrated, at length, all the insults and grievances received from their enemies within her recollection, concluding by declaring that, in her judgment, war was the only alternative. The women unanimously declared their opinion to be the same. The men next discussed the subject, and after a short time spent in talking it over, they declared that however unwilling they might have been before to engage in war, now, since the *women had called upon them to fight*, shame, if nothing else, should induce them to do so."

The ground of the importance attached to the feelings of women in regard to war, is their supposed power of causing, by witchcraft, the death of their friends who go out to war, and the fear that they may desert to their relations when war actually begins, in case their sympathies are with them.

" *Friday, February 21st.*—These people having so far advanced in fortifying their town as to render it safe to leave, determined to make an attack on Grahway to-day. It having rained in the morning, they did not get off until two or three o'clock this afternoon. Having reached Grahway, they manœuvred before it for more than an hour, with the view of drawing out the Grahwayans from their entrenchments. As, however, they declined coming out, and it was too late to make an assault upon the town, the Cavalla people returned home.

" *Saturday, February 22d.*—This morning, at seven o'clock, we were informed that our people had gone to renew their attack on Grahway. The largest body took the same direction as yesterday, through the woods, so as to appear suddenly before the town. As soon as they appeared in the meadow, the smaller division advanced to join them, and the whole shortly presented themselves before Grahway. The people there manifested the same indisposition to come out that they did yesterday, but finding, at length, that a battle was unavoidable, they sallied forth to meet their enemies. Both parties drew up near to each other, and remained for some time in this position, as if each feared to strike the first blow. During this time, being near enough together to be distinctly heard, they continued to menace, ridicule and curse each other in the most offensive language which they could command ; still no gun was fired—no movement towards an attack made, on either side. It was now eleven o'clock. At this time, the wife of ' Nypra,' the war-man, made her appearance suddenly, between the hostile armies, and, advancing to her husband, thus addressed him : ' Nypra, why have you kept these Cavalla people so long here without food ? Do you not know that I can eat nothing until you have burned these towns ; and why do you wait ? Do you not see, already, the sky filled with smoke and flame from the burning towns ? On! and do your work.' Nypra made no reply, but taking his wife by the arm, paced with her backwards and forwards between the hostile armies, looking all the while intently upon a small looking-glass which he always takes with him. During all this time, he was near enough to be shot by the opposite party, who, indeed, continually threatened to fire. He, how-

ever, heeded them not, until, at length, having finished
his incantations, at a given signal, there was a general
onset by the Cavalla people. In fifteen minutes, their
enemies were retreating before them, and Grahway was
in flames. Some twenty-five Grahway people were left
dead on the field, and nearly as many were wounded.
Two small towns besides Grahway were also burned, and
nearly all the property in them, except what was consumed by the flames, fell into the hands of the Cavalla
people. The loss of this people was five killed and some
six or eight wounded. It was truly a melancholy and
heathen spectacle, to see, as I stood on Dodo-Luh point
with Mr. Hening, our people, returning with their dead
and wounded, and bearing, with shouts of exultation,
the heads of their slaughtered foes. Eighteen of these
they piled on a high rock on the sea-shore, that they
might have the barbarous satisfaction of beholding them
as they passed."

Five weeks elapsed after this battle before another
encounter, during which interval the Sabbath services
were regularly held and attended by good congregations.
On the 31st of March, Mr. Payne again writes :

" An eventful day to us at Cavalla ! At five o'clock
this morning we were awakened by such a discharge of
fire-arms as left no doubt that we were in the midst of
war. The long expected attack had been made, simul-
taneously, by the River Cavalla and Grahway people, on
the two small towns of Cavalla, in the direction of those
two places respectively. * * * * * * * * * * *
In all, twenty-five men have fallen to-day; and since
the beginning of the existing difficulties not fewer than

one hundred, on both sides; a degree of mortality unprecedented in the history of this tribe, or indeed of any
others in its neighborhood."

"*Thursday, April 4th.*—This morning, at seven
o'clock, there was a general 'turn out' of the soldiers
of this place, for the purpose of purifying themselves
after the battle of Monday. This is always done on the
fourth day after fighting. Before the peculiar ceremony
which constitutes the purification, they went through
the evolutions performed in war, and then arranged themselves in a line along the sea shore. Here, after a general discharge of their arms, all walked in far enough to
allow the waves to lave their feet, and were thus purified.

"*Saturday, April 6th.*—Late on last Monday night,
after I had recorded the events of the day, we heard
great rejoicing in town. On asking the cause, we were
informed that the River people had sent to 'beg.' This
was equivalent to saying they *had been beaten;* and
hence the noise we now heard.

"Two women, natives of this place, but married at
the River towns, were the messengers sent to 'beg' for
peace. They brought in their hands a copper rod,
which, however, as well as any thing else used for this
purpose, is called tweh (axe); this latter being the most
sacred, and indeed, the appropriate token on such occasions. The messengers first presented themselves at the
gate of the small town next to the river, using the most
humilating language. They were kept *standing* there
until information of their arrival was brought to the
headmen of the large town. These sent word to them,
that they could not enter town, but must go back home,

and bring the proper 'tweh.' They accordingly went back, but returned the same night, presenting themselves again at the gate. But, once more, they were sent home. The next morning they came again, bringing the proper 'tweh.' They were then admitted into the large town, and as they passed through to the assembly-house of the 'Sedibo,' cried aloud, 'A ya tweho! A ya tweho! (we bring the axe,) W. S. K. (the name of the headman,) you have beaten us; we are not equal to you; you have our lands—our homes—we have come to beg them from your hands.' The 'tweh' was then received and hung up in the top of the Sedibo's house, as a memorial that these people had been beaten and begged them. The women then returned home.

"On the following day, the same two women came again, accompanied by two men from the River towns. The latter brought with them some tiger's teeth as a present to the Tibawa, or head of the Sedibo. The people now generally assembled to meet these messengers at the Sedibo's house. One of the old men of this place then rose, and gave a detailed account of the relation of the Cavalla and River people, from the settlement of the latter in their present towns. He dwelt particularly on the fact, that the land on which the River people had built their towns was given them by the Cavalla people, and of their ingratitude in attempting to wrest more from them now. Now, however, they had not only failed in their attempt, but been beaten in war. He then reminded the delegates, that their people had threatened, in case they beat the Cavalla people, to make them go back to Rocktown, whence they came; and, as *they* had been beaten, it was only pursuing a policy originated by them, to insist that they should return to Cape Palmas and Grahway, from whence they had emigrated. And this he called Gnisreah (God) to witness, was the only condition upon which his people would conclude peace.

"The delegates, in reply, acknowledged that their people had been beaten, and that they were now forced to come and beg their lands from their conquerors ; but said that they could not think of abandoning their homes. All this, the delegates were forced to say *sitting*, while the speaker of this people *stood*, in token of superiority. Neither party would, however, recede from the ground which they had taken, though a long and angry discussion was maintained on both sides.   Notwithstanding this, they proceeded to make peace in the usual manner, described about a month ago.   Then followed a most singular part of the ceremony, with which the whole concluded.   The River Cavalla delegates, after having ' spit water,' seized two pieces of wood, and ran through the town in every direction for the purpose of killing any fowls which they might chance to see.   Having, at length, killed two in this manner, they took them home to be eaten there.

"This same ceremony was performed at the River, by two men sent from this place.   Still it seems that the matter was not fully settled.   It would appear, indeed, that the ' begging' party in such cases, is obliged to continue to give until the conquerors say ' enough.' Accordingly, to-day, the River people sent a cow, further to propitiate these people.   It was received ; but the same conditions for a final settlement were repeated that were proposed a few days ago. Whether this is a mere threat, made to extort as much as possible from the supplicants, or it is intended really to be carried into effect, remains to be seen."

CHAPTER XXXII.

No further disturbances occurred during the year, and the affairs of the station resumed their wonted course. The congregations on the Sabbath continued to increase, and among them were a number of women. The females had appeared, from custom and force of circumstances, to be in a great measure excluded from religious influence, until Mrs. Payne and Mrs. Patch adopted the plan of visiting them on Saturday afternoons, conversing with them familiarly on their spiritual interests, and urging their attendance on public worship. The result of this effort was most encouraging, many being induced to become regular hearers of the Word of Life, and evincing much interest in the truths thus proclaimed.

Mr. Payne's journal of November 26th, contains the following interesting incident :

" A curious native ceremony, connected with the late war, terminated to-day. It appears that war is considered in itself so evil a thing, that it invariably leaves upon the land where it has been carried on a blighting influence, called ' gla ;' this, if not removed, prevents or mars all the productions of the earth.

"War having now terminated, in the wishes and opinions of these people, and the farming season being near at hand, it had become necessary that this 'gla' should be taken away. Accordingly, a man living at Garaway, some forty miles to the windward, skilled in this art, was sent for. He arrived several days ago, but the ceremony did not begin until Sunday night. At that time, the crier went through the town, calling upon all the population to remain at home on the following day. In the morning, the solemn season commenced. No one was permitted to leave the place for another, and all strangers arriving, were required to remain for three days, during which the ceremony was to continue.

"The purifier now commenced his work. Having gone to the 'bush,' he brought some leaves, which he beat up in a mortar. He then put in cassada, palm nuts, rice, and all the fruits of the earth that were at hand, pounding them with the leaves. This mixture he took and scattered over the fields of cassada and vegetables near the town. He now returned to the 'Ta-kai,' or Bodias' house, in which are kept the town greegrees. A goat was brought. The purifier stood up and invoked Gnisuah, God, four times, and then the 'kwi,' departed spirits. He confessed, in the name of the people, that, contrary to their wishes, they had been involved in war, and thereby defiled the land. That war, however, was now, so far as they were concerned, terminated ; and they desired never more to be engaged in it. They now sought to cleanse their land ; and to propitiate the kwi, offered the goat. The goat was then killed, and· its blood sprinkled before the Bodias' house, when there was

a general and prolonged firing.   Thence they all set out
again, and proceeding in a tumultuous manner, returned
to the beach.   Here, again, there was a universal discharge of musketry, repeated again and again, thus sig-
nifying that they had *taken all the war out of town*, and
fired it away."

Mr. Hening had left Cavalla, on his way to Taboo,
on the 7th of March.   A few extracts from his journal
will acquaint the reader with the progress of events at
this station, while those just recorded were occurring at
Cavalla.

"It was night before we reached Taboo.   The pupils
of the school, who had been long and anxiously awaiting
our arrival, stood on the opposite bank of the river.   As
the canoe glided over the waters, their shouts of joy, and
the glare of the blazing torches in their hands, gave to
the scene a romantic interest.   The school at Taboo consisted of twelve pupils; and the manner in which they
had been trained and disciplined by their instructor, a
young native, Musu, afforded a most gratifying evidence
of his zeal and fidelity. *   *   *   *   *   *   *   *

"*March 12th.*—To-day, I have had what is called
a ' palaver ' with the natives.   This is a term which
seems to have no definite meaning, but is applied to
everything.   Early in the morning, Musu informed me
that a number of natives were assembled in the room
below, a deputation of the kings and headmen of the
surrounding towns—and that they had come to ' set the
palaver' about the price of rice, palm-oil, labor, &c.   As
the movement was one of which I had been premonished
by my brethren of the mission, I was prepared to meet

it. As soon as a ' new man' is located, the first thing
done, is, to discover, by a variety of annoying experiments upon his patience, if he has a ' strong mouth ;' or, in
other words, whether he has the firmness to resist any
species of extortion which may be practised upon him.
These experiments are repeated from time to time, subjecting the missionary to much inconvenience and har-
rassment, and are only to be put down by his maintaining
a firm and decided stand. When I went to the room
below, I found it filled with natives ; and as all were
talking, or rather shouting, at the top of their voices, the
scene of uproar and confusion is indescribable. One man
was tricked off in a military cocked hat ; another, in a
pair of huge, rusty, brass epaulettes ; a third, brandished
a broadsword in his hand ; and each one of the motley
group was equipped in some tattered, cast-off garment,
such as a night-gown, military frock coat, &c. I was
satisfied, at a glance, that the whole scene had been
studiously gotten up to impress the ' new man' with becoming ideas of its dignity and importance. ' Henni-o !'
asked the spokesman of the occasion, who had acquired
his knowledge of the Anglo-Saxon in a voyage to Liver-
pool—' Henni-o ! you see here all dis genman ? He be
big man for dis country ; all dis country he belong him ;
and now he come for talk rice-palaver.' When ' the
palaver was talked,' an exorbitant increase of price
was demanded upon every article. This I of course re-
solutely refused to give. The demand was reiterated
again and again, with like success. At length, finding
me inflexible, the discussion of the matter was postponed
to a future day, my visitors promising that, in the mean-

time, they would 'look their heads'—that is, deliberate.
As their policy was to coerce me into compliance, no
provisions of any kind were brought to my house for
several weeks.　At the expiration of that time, they returned—were again baffled—and finding that my 'mouth
was strong,' matters were settled upon a quiet basis."

"*May* 10.—To-day I received a visit from a Fetish-
man or 'Devil Doctor.'　His appearance indicated his
profession　His face was streaked with red and white
paint; his body smeared with mud and palm oil; a pro-
fusion of greegrees about his person, and a black monkey's
skin, the peculiar badge of his tribe, under his arm.
From his account of the matter, he had come upon a
most benevolent enterprize.　He informed me that Mr.
Minor had been but a short time in the country—that
witches had killed him, and that for a trifle of tobacco,
he would make me some greegrees to be placed under
my house, which would shield me from all malign influences.　He declared that he was the chief of 'devil
doctors'—that his power over the supernatural agencies
was unlimited; and as a proof of it, referred to the fact
that he had frequently cut off his own head with a cutlass, and walked about with it, a whole night, under his
arm.　He was amazed at the incredulity which I manifested, and upon my remonstrating with him upon the
folly and wickedness of his pretensions, he offered to establish them by some experiments, which would banish
all doubt from my mind.　These were deferred until a
future day, as a consultation with the devil was the
preliminary and indispensable step to success.　I heard
nothing of the devil-man for three or four weeks.　But

the eventful day arrived, and the experiments were exhibited. The pupils of my school, my family, and a number of natives from the town, were spectators. The doctor unrolled his monkey's skin, and took from it a small wooden bowl, capable of holding a pint measure. This was next filled to the brim with water, and then streaked, red and yellow, with the dye of some vegetable substances, which he had expressed by chewing. Four light sticks, about a foot long and tapering to a bulb at one extremity, were then produced; these preparations being made, a sharp-pointed piece of iron was driven into the floor, so as to stand firm and upright. The bowl was then placed upon it, as near the centre of the bottom as could be done, the equilibrium adjusted by means of the sticks—and in this position, wonderful to tell, the bowl and its contents remained balanced! The experiment done, the doctor looked around with an air of. triumph, declaring that it was the power of witchcraft. His triumph, however, was of short duration; and he retired amidst the jeers and laughter of the spectators, when I performed the same experiment, without evoking to my aid any more potent or mysterious agent than a steady hand. He determined, however, upon one more effort to retrieve his reputation. The experiment consisted in plaistering one of his legs with a quantity of thick palm oil, and causing a heated iron to pass rapidly over it without producing pain. He was again confounded, when, simply dipping my hand in water, a similar use was made of the heated iron. It is by arts like these, which scarcely rise to the dignity of legerdemain, that the Fetish-man obtains so great an ascendency over the

12

minds of his ignorant dupes. His supposed alliance with
the devil, (who is always invoked on such occasions,)
invests him with a mysterious awe, and then the most
simple feats of jugglery are played off without detection,
as the workings of a supernatural agency. Here is found
the most formidable obstacle to the advancement of the
Gospel. The intellect lies not only dormant, but para-
lized, under its weight."

"*October* 26.—This is a memorable day! I can record an event, a rich blessing on my labors, which is
enough to repay every past sacrifice or privation—Musu
has been admitted to the holy ordinance of baptism!
This of itself, would be an abundant cause for adoring
gratitude, but since his public profession of his faith in
Christ, five others, one an adult, a native man employed
in my service, and the other four pupils of my school,
have expressed the hope that their hearts have been renewed by divine grace. They are candidates for baptism, and will be admitted to the Church, should their
walk and conversation be such as to confirm the pleasing
hope that they are 'new creatures in Christ Jesus.'

"Since my residence in this country, my school has
been the object of my deepest solicitude. Withdrawn as
its pupils are, from all the corrupting influences around
them, and trained, by daily precept, in the fear and nurture of the Lord, I have always turned to it for encouragement when all else seemed dark and cheerless. May
the Lord carry on the work thus graciously begun, and
ripen to a glorious harvest, the seed sown in faith and
prayer."

Dr. Perkins and his family had remained at Mt.

Vaughan during the first three months succeeding their return from the United States, in the expectation that after so long an absence, they might be obliged to undergo a second acclimation. Such, however, was not the case, and in May they took up their abode at Taboo, designing to remain with Mr. and Mrs. Hening until a comfortable dwelling could be erected at Rockbookah, where they were to be stationed. Mrs. Perkins took charge of a class of girls, and the Doctor devoted himself to the practice of his profession among the natives. His medical report mentions the fact, that in the course of six months, he had treated upwards of three hundred cases. It is evident that the people are not only willing, but anxious to receive medical treatment; and the importance of this profession in conciliating their good will, and thus opening a channel for religious influence, can hardly be over-estimated. In December, Dr. Perkins removed to Rockbookah, and re-opened that station, which had been left vacant since Mr. Appleby's departure for the United States, in 1843.

At Fishtown, the result of the year's exertions was encouraging. The school was in full operation and well attended in both departments. Dr. Savage makes particular mention of Nimleh, Samuel Boyd, his most advanced scholar among the boys. This young man had been under the care of the missionaries of the American Board until their removal to the Gaboon river, when he was transferred to our own Mission. His progress in his studies had been highly satisfactory, and at the quarterly examination, held in September, 1845, he is reported as having recited creditably in arithmetic as far as frac-

tions, astronomy and geography, besides showing good
specimens of writing and composition. A further notice
of him, extracted from Dr. Savage's journal, will be of
interest to the reader.

"*July* 24*th*.—Nimleh, my oldest male scholar, came
to me this morning, saying that he had been trying to
reconcile an apparent discrepancy between the Creed
and the Gospel. The Creed said that Christ rose from
the dead and ascended into heaven ; how is it, then,
that he was on the earth some time after he rose, and did
many wonderful things ? Did he descend again to his
disciples ? * * * * * * * * * * * *

"*Sunday morning, September* 14*th*.—Nimleh, who
acts as my interpreter, came to me, with evident pertur-
bation, saying that the people of Middletown have
threatened to poison him for interpreting, faithfully, my
words in preaching. This gave me a good opportunity
to explain to him several expressions of our Saviour, the
meaning of which he had asked before, such as, ' A
man's foes shall be they of his own household.' ' He
that seeks to save his life, shall lose it.' ' I came not to
send peace on the earth, but a sword,' &c., &c. I asked
him how he felt when he heard such threats from his
own people. He replied, ' They trouble me but little,
when I remember that Christ has forewarned us of
these things.' I asked him if he thought he would be
willing to die by poison, if God should permit it. He
replied very promptly, ' Yes, sir.' His growth in grace
has of late been quite perceptible.

"*November* 16*th*.—Nimleh asked me this morning,
' if sinners in hell could see saints in heaven ; and if the

Abraham whom the rich man in hell saw afar off, was the Abraham who begat Isaac ?' He asked also, ' if we should carry the same wills into the other world that we have here ?' meaning, if we should have equal powers of volition there, and liberty to carry out our wills into action. In the same connection, he asked if a desire to sin, though it be not accomplished, will be punished by God. He seemed easily to comprehend the difference between evil desires cherished, and such desires promptly suppressed from fear and love to God."

CHAPTER XXXIII.

Review of the year 1845—Arrival of the Rev. Mr. Messenger—Illness and death of Mrs. Patch.

CHRISTMAS-DAY, 1845, the ninth anniversary of the establishment of the Mission, marked an era of great prosperity in its annals. Five stations were now occupied, a missionary and his wife residing at each. The number of laborers in the field was greater than at any former period, and, with the exception of intermittents and other slight ails, there had been no sickness among them during the year. Wherever the Gospel had been preached, it had proved the power of God unto salvation to some believing soul ; several had been added to the Church at the different stations, and the indirect influence of Christianity was evident, in various ways, upon the mass of the people.

The whole extent of sea-coast embraced in the operations of the Mission, was more than fifty miles, and the number of pupils one hundred and fifty.

As it was desirable that the Christmas festival should be duly observed at the several stations, the annual meeting was postponed until the 30th, when the gentlemen met at Cavalla, and after the transaction of business, the anniversary sermon was preached by the Rev. Mr. Hening. It was an occasion of devout joy and thankfulness, and when, a few weeks later, the little band was yet farther enlarged by the arrival of the Rev. E. J. P. Messenger, all hearts beat high with renewed hopes of still growing prosperity. It is painful, indeed, to be obliged to reverse the picture ; but God, in infinite wisdom, saw fit severely to check these glowing anticipations. In these disappointed hopes, this exchange of sunshine for cloud, and joy for heaviness, we read, however, only a repetition of the lesson which is stamped on all below ; and we beg the reader, while he goes with us again to the bedside of the dying, and again mourns with us over scenes of trial and bereavement, not to forget that the African Mission has known seasons of prosperity as well as of adversity, and that often, when most tried in outward circumstances, its faithful servants were permitted to rejoice in those spiritual blessings for which they would joyfully endure a tenfold suffering.

The warmest part of the year had now arrived, and the heat became unusually intense. Much sickness prevailed among the natives and colonists, and the health of all the missionaries was more or less impaired. On the 8th of March Mrs. Patch was attacked by serious illness, and on the 18th expired. She had been a faithful servant of the Church, and the reader will be interested in such memorials of her life and death as we have been able to collect.

Catharine Low Lyon was the daughter of Enoch Lyon, of Newport, R. I., and was born in Boston, June 3d, 1812. In 1823, her parents moved to Lowell, where she became interested in the Episcopal Church, **and was** received into its communion, by baptism, on the 8th **of** June, 1828, by the Rev. Theodore Edson. She received confirmation from the hands of the Rt. Rev. Bishop Griswold, on the 23d of the same month.

At the age of twenty-two, she was united in marriage with Mr. William Patch, a devoted member of the Episcopal Church, and an ardent friend of the African Mission. For some time before his death, it had been Mr. Patch's desire to devote himself to the service of Christ on that heathen shore ; but God had other designs for him, and, on the 11th of April, 1842, he was summoned from the labors of earth to the rest of heaven. His bereaved widow, who had fully sympathised in his desire to promote the kingdom of Christ in Africa, resolved to consecrate her remaining years to the work which he had loved, and having made application to the Board, received her appointment in the spring of 1844.

Speaking of the parting scene, when she took leave of her family in Lowell, she says : " I thought my friends all seemed more sad and silent than the case required. I almost wavered once, but it was only for a moment. I thought of Africa, and that I had given myself to the work, which soon brought back my wandering affections.

" I think my present situation in life has, by the providence of God, been brought about by a long chain of events, which I can trace to my earliest recollections, when the first germ of a missionary spirit was implanted in my mind. I remember very distinctly the instructions received in the Sunday School, when I was quite **a** little girl. There was one principle which my teacher tried to inculcate, to be good myself and try to do good to others."

In her journal, written at sea, she mentions having suffered much from sea-sickness, and writes: "I felt that in God was my only trust. My native land was fast receding from my view; I might never behold it again; yet I felt happy, calm, even joyful. Yes, L——, you would not shed one tear if you knew how happy I feel. Christ can and does give me strength in every hour of need. It is sweet to trust entirely to Him ' who layeth the beams of his chambers in the waters, who maketh the clouds his chariot, and walketh upon the wings of the wind.' "

Of the voyage and her arrival on the African coast, we have already given notices, extracted from her own journal, which brings up her history until the time when she entered upon her duties as teacher of the Female School at Cavalla. " In the performance of these," says Mr. Payne, " she continued with the exception of a single day, until her last sickness. In her sincere devotion, the untiring zeal and perseverance with which she sought to improve the children of her charge, she was indeed an example worthy of all imitation. As a member of the family circle, her character was very estimable. Quiet, meek, cheerful, she felt herself, and desired to make others feel, that we are members one of another, and are associated together to bless, and be blessed by one another. Thus passed away nearly eighteen months, scarcely interrupted by a day's serious indisposition. Her good health, indeed, was a matter of surprise to all. She

12*

would, it is true, sometimes complain of unpleasant feelings, on account of which she was advised to take medicines. She had, however, been so unused to sickness, that she appeared incapable of estimating the importance of taking proper remedies ; and this, Dr. Perkins thinks, was a great error, and laid the foundation of her final attack, which came with such accumulated strength as to baffle the power of medicines.

" On Saturday, March 7th, after making her usual visit to the native women, for the purpose of conversing with them and inducing them to attend services on the coming Sabbath, she felt so unwell that she immediately retired. On Sunday morning, however, she thought herself so much better that she dressed herself with the view of going to church, but the effort proved too much for her strength, and she again retired. On Monday morning, after taking calomel the night before, she appeared to have so little fever that we gave her tonics. In the afternoon, she was again more unwell, but did not think herself seriously so. This opinion she stated to Mrs. Payne, remarking at the same time, that should it prove otherwise, her trust was in God, who, she felt sure, could give strength for any emergency. Her disorder continuing on Tuesday, we determined to send for Dr. Perkins the next morning. He came as soon as he could possibly do so, and at once pronounced her most seriously diseased, her liver being evidently very much affected. The most active remedies were at once resorted to, and continued until her death, without, however, producing the least apparent effect. Still, so robust had been her health, that the doctor continued to hope for her recovery.

" During the greater portion of her illness, her mind was so much under the influence either of disease or medicines, that she was indisposed to converse. She once, however, remarked to Mrs. Payne, that though naturally averse to talking about her feelings, she thought a great deal.

" On ascertaining that she was dangerously ill, I went up to her room on Sunday morning. She appeared much gratified to see me. On my remarking that she appeared very sick, she replied, ' Yes, but God has been very merciful to me." After reading a portion of Scripture, and praying, at the close of which exercise she pronounced, most distinctly, Amen, she begged that I would come often to visit her, and expressed the wish that we would inform her as soon as we should think there was a probability of a fatal termination to her disease ; at the same time remarking, that if it was the will of God, she would ' be happy to die.'

" On Monday, I again read and prayed with her, but she appeared indisposed to talk.

" The next day, she was so uncomfortable that it was thought unadvisable for Mr. Payne to visit her ; and on the following morning, the doctor considered her symptoms so unfavorable as to render her recovery exceedingly doubtful. According to her request, Mr. Payne acquainted her with this opinion. ' She appeared,' he writes, ' somewhat surprised at the information, remarking that she felt no worse. I asked if she had any special message to her friends at home or elsewhere. She

replied that there was nothing particular that she could
think of, and then ejaculated, ' Oh, God ! my times are
in thy hands.'

" The few observations which she made appeared to
call forth so much effort, that I thought it inexpedient
to trouble her with more questions.   During the morning, however, the nurse being alone with her, she prayed
most fervently for God's blessing upon the Mission, the
people, and especially upon the children whom she had
instructed.   After this, she seemed unable to speak, and
to be, for the most part, insensible to things around her.
But, thank God ! she needed not a dying hour to prepare her to meet her God.   She had 'set,' and kept
' her house in order,' and, as her quiet spirit withdrew
gradually from its decaying tenement, it ' was carried by
angels into Abraham's bosom.'

" Early the next morning, many of the natives, according to their custom, visited Mr. and Mrs. Payne, to
condole with them on their loss, and to take a last look
of their departed friend.   Services were held in the
school-house, and the body laid in its last resting-place,
beside the grave of the Rev. L. B. Minor.

" Both on this occasion, and on the following Sabbath, Mr. Payne endeavored to improve the sad event by
contrasting the death of the righteous, thus quietly
sinking to his rest, with the distress and dread experienced by the heathen at the approach of death.   That
the contrast was felt and acknowledged, was evidenced
by the remark of one of his auditors : ' Such a manner
of death,' said she, ' I cannot comprehend.'

CHAPTER XXXIV.

AFTER a week of close and anxious attendance at the bedside of Mrs. Patch, Dr. Perkins returned to his station. What must have been his feelings when he found his wife lying dangerously ill with yellow fever! This disease is one of the most formidable to which the acclimated resident is exposed ; but, in the present case, by the blessing of God, it was promptly arrested, and Mrs. Perkins was soon restored to convalescence.

But the hand of the destroyer was not yet stayed. On the 20th of March, Mr. Messenger was attacked by the acclimating fever, which terminated fatally on the ninth day. The account of his last hours will be best given in the words of his attendant physician, Dr. Savage, by whom the following letter was addressed to the Secretary of the Board.

" FISHTOWN, *April* 1*st,* 1846.

" By my last dates, you were informed of our gratification at the unexpected arrival of the Rev. E. J. P. Messenger. The melancholy duty now devolves upon me, of informing you of his sickness and death.

"On the 28th of January, he came to Fishtown, at the desire of the Mission, to be under my charge, while passing through the first stages of his acclimation. Here he remained more than seven weeks, during which time he expressed himself, daily, as well, with the occasional exception of an affection of the back, to which he had been subjected for several years, and from which he suffered more or less pain and inconvenience. Having not yet seen all the members of the Mission, and desiring very much to be present at our regular meeting, to be held at Cavalla on the 26th of March, he left Fishtown on the morning of the 20th, for Mt. Vaughan, designing to preach the funeral sermon, on Sunday, of a colonist communicant, and, on the Wednesday following, proceed to Cavalla. He rode on horseback from this to Rocktown, a distance of about six miles, which place he desired to visit, with a view to a decision either for or against it as his future station ; thence he went, in my boat, by sea, to Cape Palmas, distant, in a straight line, about four miles. He was made very sick by the motion of the boat, and, which I regretted to hear, declined the use of the awning, and of his umbrella. On arriving at Cape Palmas, he complained much of his back ; and, on that account, preferred walking to riding, most of the way to Mt. Vaughan.

Soon after he left us, a note arrived from Mr. Payne, informing me that Mrs. Perkins was ill at Rockbookah. Thinking that Dr. Perkins might be enfeebled by his close attendance on Mrs. Patch during her last sickness, and therefore would need my assistance, I started early next morning, Saturday, in my boat, for Cavalla, whence

I proceeded, by land, immediately to Rockbookah, where I arrived just after dark, on the same day. I was greatly relieved to find Mrs. Perkins in a favorable state, though not out of danger, and Dr. Perkins very well. While at family prayers, the next morning, a man arrived from Mt. Vaughan with a note, stating that Mr. Messenger was attacked with fever. Feeling it my duty to go at once, I started immediately after breakfast, and travelling the whole day, in a clear hot sun, I reached the bedside of our sick brother at dark ; having spent the Lord's day as I had never before done in Africa. I found nothing alarming in his case, and he continued in about the same state for the following three days—no material change occurring in his symptoms. Great torpor of the system existed from the outset, which, in all such cases, is decidedly unfavorable. Medicines would not produce their specific effect. On the seventh day from his attack a crisis occurred, when the powers of life began to fail. Gradually declining, he expired on the ninth day.

"Mr. Messenger's case is an anomalous one in my experience. It was, very clearly, a complicated one. What the precise nature of his dorsal affection was, primarily, I am not prepared to say. His physician in Philadelphia pronounced it to be lumbago, and therefore it would be no obstacle in his coming to Africa. In case it were simply lumbago, I should have given the same opinion. On his arrival at Mt. Vaughan, he complained much of his back, and made known to Mrs. Appleby that, the night before leaving Fishtown, he had slept with his window open, and, a tornado arising, the wind

blew directly and strongly upon him the whole night.
He seemed to think that, whatever his dorsal affection
might be, it would be the main cause of his death, and
spoke several times, during his sickness, of suffering
acutely from it.   Whether it was primarily lumbago or
not, I cannot say; but one thing was evident, that the
symptoms then existing indicated an acute affection
within the spinal canal—I should say, 'spinal meringti-
tis,' or inflammation in the membranes investing the
spinal cord.

"Great restlessness and irritation were attendant
throughout, but his mind was clear and active till within the last eighteen or twenty hours, when he became
delirious, and expired, as we thought, in that condition.

"It now remains for me to speak of his state of mind
under sickness, and in view of death.   And here I would
remark, that, from the first, he manifested a calmness
and patience under suffering, that seemed to all, beautifully illustrative of his piety.   His conversation and
whole demeanor in view of the approach of death, were
more like those of a man about entering upon a moment-
ous journey, rather than his departure for the other
world.   The following is the substance of my notes,
made as the facts transpired.

"*March 26th, Thursday.*—A change for the worse
has been perceived since two P. M.; his pulse, from
that time, has indicated extreme danger and approaching dissolution.   At half-past five P. M. I sat down by
his side, with a heavy heart, for now only had my hopes
began to fail, and asked if his spiritual comfort was affected by his illness.   He replied that his feelings, in this

respect, were peculiarly pleasant, though he did not know but that it was owing in some measure to the excitement of medicine. He remarked that he had been in a cold, lifeless state, owing probably to a protracted, unpleasant voyage, which sometimes led him almost to doubt whether he had any interest in Christ. I then repeated, 'Look unto me and be ye saved.' He immediately replied, 'O yes, I have often thought upon that text, and it has brought comfort to my soul. I think I can say that if I am taken away, I shall be with Christ. I rely wholly upon him ; he is my support.' This he said with marked fervor, and then added, 'But I suppose I ought not to talk much.'

" *Friday morning, half-past four.*—He remarked that he felt a sinking internally, which told him that he could not rally, and asked my opinion of his state and prospects. I replied that great uncertainty attended the diseases of this country ; that I had seen persons, apparently sicker than he was, recover ; but still that I had felt, for two days past, that there was increasing danger in his case ; an obstinacy of symptoms existing for which I could not account, and medicines failing to produce their usual effect. He seemed to study my countenance as I spoke, and replied, apparently with great composure, 'Well, I have no desire on the subject, but leave it in God's hands, to live or die. I thought that in coming to Africa I was in the path of duty, and that I could be happy in no other field of labor. My mind is still unchanged, and should I now be taken away, I can see no reason for regretting that I came. My feelings, in view of death, are those of happiness, and the only re-

gret I can have, is the discouraging effect it may have
on others.' I then remarked that, as the result could
not be foreseen, if he had any requests to leave in the
event of death, it would be well to do it at an early period. He then desired to be affectionately remembered
to certain individuals, giving their names and residences ;
then to the children of the Sunday-school of the Church
of the Epiphany in Philadelphia ; to the ladies of the
Sewing Society of the same church, and to the members
of the Foreign Committee. To the children of the Sunday-school of the Epiphany he sent an especial message :
' Tell them all to prepare to meet me in heaven. *Some*
I hope to meet, but tell them I want to meet them *all*
in that happy place.' In a subsequent conversation, I
said, ' From your remark, that the only regret you can
have in case of your death, is the discouraging effect it
may exert upon others, I infer that it is your opinion
that the Mission should still be energetically sustained.
' O yes !' was the quick reply, and there was a fervor in
the language of the dying man that gave to the sentiment, in my mind, the solemnity and importance of eternity. I confess that when one and another of our number falls, or withdraws, there is a possibility, if not a
probability, that our labors will result in failure ; *only,
however*, through *its discouraging effect upon others.*
Conceive, then, if you can, what strength and encour
agement such declarations bring home to our hearts.
' O yes !' he continued, ' a great work has already been
done, and a greater still is to be done. I have looked
upon it as, by far, the most interesting Mission of the
Church, and now second only to China ; yes, it ought

to be sustained, but *where are the men to come from ?'*
'From God,' was my only reply.   'Yes, from God,'
continued he; 'the Lord will raise them up when it is
time to do it.'   *   *   *   *   *   *   *   *   *   *

"On Friday afternoon he entertained the idea that
he should rally and recover, but, before night, he gave
up all such hope.   At half-past six, he exclaimed, 'O
for grace for a dying hour!   I then repeated some texts,
such as, 'Ask and ye shall receive'—'Look unto me and
be saved'—'As thy day, so shall thy strength be,' &c.
He replied, 'Tell the children of your school, that that
is my message to them, 'Look unto me and be ye
saved.'   I have told them that again and again, and
now I find it my only support.   Give my love to Mrs.
Savage, and tell her to persevere in faith, and her reward will come hereafter.'   I continued to repeat such
passages as I thought appropriate, to which he added,
with fervor, 'And, casting all thy care upon the Lord,
for he careth for thee.'

"At another time, with his arms extended upon the
bed, and looking upward, he said, 'Ah, here I lie, a poor,
weak, unprofitable servant, weak in body and mind.'   I
asked, 'Can you not lean upon the arm of the Lord, an
everlasting arm, now extended to you?'   He quickly
answered, 'O yes, I do lean upon it!' and then, after a
short pause, 'I cast all my care upon the Lord, for he
careth for me.'   Again, 'O, it is a comforting thought
that I shall leave all my sins behind!'

"I read, at intervals, selected passages from the
eighth chapter of Romans.   When I came to the 38th
and 39th verses, 'For I am persuaded that neither

death nor life shall be able to separate us from the love of God which is in Christ Jesus,' he responded fervently and impressively, 'Amen.' After some moments of apparent meditation and prayer, he turned to me, with a sweet expression of countenance, and said, 'Read to me some more of those precious promises.' I then read selections from the fourteenth chapter of St. John and the 27th Psalm, in which he seemed to take delight.

"Again, after repeating the 25th and 26th verses of the 11th chapter of St. John's Gospel, 'I am the resurrection and the life; he that believeth in me, though he were dead, yet shall he live, and whosoever liveth and believeth in me, shall never die'—I said, 'Believest thou this?' He replied, with great solemnity, 'I believe; Lord, help thou my unbelief!'

"At another time, he said, 'I know that Jesus Christ died for me, and on this I rely!'

"Throughout Friday, he was very free in conversation, and highly edifying. To Mrs. Appleby, who showed, in many ways, the kindness and unwearied sympathy of a Christian woman, as she endeavored to restrain him from too much talking, he said, 'I feel that I must talk; my time is short, and I must spend it for Christ; we ought to do all we can to glorify him who has done so much for us.' Much more was said, but surely this is enough for all who knew him, to show that he died glorying in the Cross.

"Mr. Messenger expired at twenty minutes past four on Saturday morning.

"*March 28th*, 1846.—Dr. Savage adds, 'The close was a painful scene, and did I not believe that the powers of life, the susceptibilities of the system were ob-tainded, or mercifully reduced at such a moment, I should say that his corporeal sufferings were extreme.

"In what we know of his life, and in his last sick-ness, we have good hope in his death; we doubt not that he is accepted with God in the Beloved, and there-fore, that our loss is his greatest gain. I can bear full testimony to his Christian character while he was a member of my family. In all his intercourse with us and the native population around us, he shed the sweet fragrance of a life wholly given to God. All in our household and schools loved him; and I do not believe there is an eye among us which has not paid its sincere tribute to his cherished memory. Sobs were heard, and tears flowed, while, on the morning after his burial, Sunday, I delivered to the assembled schools his dying message, 'Look unto me and be ye saved.' I have told them this again and again, and now I find it my sup-port. It was a truly impressive occasion. Only two weeks before, he whose dying words I was then deliver-ing, stood in that very place, apparently in perfect health, entreating that very auditory to flee unto Christ and be saved. His past exhortations and instructions came up to the mind with effect, and I cannot doubt that the blessing of God will follow his brief labors among us. The impression he made upon the native population around us may, in some degree, be appre-hended, from the fact that, on my return from Mt. Vaughan, the old Chief and his most influential head-men waited upon me, and expressed their sympathy at the loss of my brother; and others of subordinate rank did the same, all as one saying, 'Ah, that was a good man.'"

CHAPTER XXXV.

IT is not to be supposed that the remaining members of the little missionary band, thus afflicted and bereaved, should be unmoved by these repeated trials; but their chief anxiety was, as Mr. Messenger's had been, lest the Church at home should be discouraged. The Rev. Mr. Hening expressed the sentiments of all his associates, when he wrote as follows : " This visitation of an all-wise Providence has produced among us no feeling of despondency, no relaxation of effort. Indeed, when we behold our comrades thus falling by our side, and realize the frail tenure of our own lives, the motive becomes more urgent to do, with all our might, the work which is before us. All that we ask is, that the Church shall remain faithful to her responsibilities ; if those whom she has sent to lead a forlorn hope fall with their armor around them, let her commission others for the contest."

The same missionary records, as evidence of the encouragement which still cheered them in the midst of their trials, the baptism of five native converts at his own station, on one occasion. This interesting event took place at Easter, April 12th, 1846, and several instances are given of the faithfulness and zeal of these young disciples. On the same day, an adult Krooman, who had embraced the faith of the Gospel under circumstances of peculiar trial, was baptized at Fishtown ; and a few months later, Mr. Payne admitted to the congregation of Christ's flock, three of the pupils at Cavalla. O! if one soul exceed in value the wealth of the whole world, was not all that had been done and suffered amply repaid ?

After mentioning some who had been trained in the Mission schools and were now employed as assistants and teachers, Mr. Payne remarks : "Nor does a view of such as have been qualified for teachers, show all that has been accomplished by the Mission schools. They have been the means of raising up the assistants, who in various capacities relieve the missionaries, and by their example, as well as employment, give form and strength to the cause of Christianity and civilization. In the place of an illiterate, heathen interpreter and translator, I have an educated and Christian one. Instead of having to purchase provisions for the station, as at first, at the sacrifice of one half of my valuable time, to serve tables, all this is now done by a Christian native. One youth, by devoting his attention to a mechanical department during the hours of labor required from all the pupils, has become quite a good carpenter. He repairs the houses on the Mission premises, and, with the exception of thatching, has built entirely four houses, inhabited by native youths, now grown to adult years and married. Another, formerly a member of the boarding school, in connexion with an adult native communicant, carries on a blacksmith's forge on the premises. In this are made a variety of articles needed in the Mission, and also such tools as are used by the natives in tilling their rice fields. These things are exchanged for rice for the use of the Mission, at such a price as to pay the artisan, and also the expenses of the shop; so that two families are supported, and a useful trade introduced, without any expense to the Mission, and but little to the missionary."

The fact here referred to, that pupils had grown up under the instruction of the missionaries, are now marrying and settling down around the stations, thus forming the nucleus of *Christian* towns, is full of promise to the next generation.

In December of this year, Dr. Savage was compelled, by continued ill health, to resign his station and withdraw permanently from the Mission. Dr. Perkins and his wife took charge of the station at Fishtown, and Mr. and Mrs. Appleby removed to Rockbookah, leaving the school at Mt. Vaughan in the care of Mrs. Thompson, who had recently returned from a visit to the United States.

In November, 1847, the Rev. Mr Hening, having been thrice brought to the verge of the grave by repeated attacks of fever, was compelled to seek renewed strength in his native land. We cannot better conclude this little volume than by an extract from an Address delivered by him before the Virginia Convention, at Norfolk, June, 1848.

' It cannot be expected that an enterprize like this, should present an unvarying aspect. It has its lights and its shadows—its periods of prosperity and of adversity. Our Mission has passed through many seasons of depression—I would, therefore, the more earnestly urge upon the Church the grounds of encouragement.

" I would notice as the first ground of encouragement, that no opposition whatever, either political or religious, is offered to the preaching of the Gospel. Compared with other Missions of the Church, ours is, in this respect, peculiarly favored. In China and Constantinople the Gospel has to encounter the hostility of a bigoted and intolerant priesthood. In Greece it meets with uncompromising opposition from the jealousies of the civil government. But, as wedded as the African is to his superstitions, he permits them to be assailed without resentment. Neither the missionary nor the converts have, at any time, been called to suffer persecution. We are fully at liberty to present the truth to their minds in the way of God's appointment. What though that truth has as yet produced but little effect upon the heart and conscience! Can we doubt that it will ultimately prove the power of God unto salvation? Do not the Scriptures assure us that ' faith cometh by hearing,' and that the preached Word is ' the sword of the Spirit?' In the free use then, of a means which God himself has ordained, we may confidently look for a blessing. And in some instances, my brethren, that blessing has been obtained. Yes! the African has been converted! The chain which Infinite Mercy has let down, has reached the profoundest abyss of mental and moral degradation. And if along that chain one, aye! but one, immortal and benighted spirit, has regained its pathway to heaven, who shall count the multitude who shall yet join in the triumphal song of the Lamb: ' Thou hast redeemed unto

13

God by thy blood, out of every tongue, and kindred, and
people, and nation, and has made us kings and priests
unto God.'

" I would notice as another ground of encouragement,
that we have free access to the infant mind. Parents readily place their children under the instruction of the missionaries, and in doing so, they often make use of expressions like these : ' *We* are too old to change our customs, but we give you our children; take *them* and
teach them what you please.' It is true, that the parents
have no higher motive than to have their children qualified, by a knowledge of English, to act as tradesmen ;
but be the motive what it may, the result is the same.
The child, once received into the Mission school, becomes
a participant in all the blessings of a Christian education.
He is trained up ' in the nurture and admonition of the
Lord,' and instances are frequent, where this early training has resulted in permanent, religious conviction.   Until the truth has had its influence upon their hearts, we
are liable to lose these pupils, through the anxiety of
their parents to make their knowledge of the English
available in trade; but when once brought under the
power of the Gospel, their attachments to the Mission
remains firm and constant, and neither threats nor per-
suasions can induce them to leave it.   I cannot too
strongly urge upon the Church the importance of affording to these young converts facilities for pursuing their
studies in the higher branches of learning and theology.
The training of a native ministry has always been regarded as an object of paramount importance, by those
acquainted with the nature of this field.   For this pur-

pose, a High-school should at once be established. There are several young men at the different stations, not only willing, but anxiously waiting to enter upon such a course of study.

"It has been my privilege to place the baptismal seal upon some of these young converts. They have manifested their sincerity by their zeal for the conversion of their countrymen. They have persevered in their efforts, undaunted by ridicule, and, in some instances, by threatened persecution. On one occasion, I despatched my trade-man to Bassa, on business connected with my station. On his return, I questioned him as to incidents of his journey, and I was delighted to find that he had not only carried his Bible with him, and introduced the subject of religion wherever business had called him, but had even gone a half-day's journey out of his way, to make known to his benighted countrymen ' the unsearchable riches of Christ.' One of the companions of Hini's journey related to me the following incident He said, that a native became so incensed at Hini's remonstrances against the folly and wickedness of his superstitions, that he came, by night, to the hut in which he lodged, with the intention of beating him. The fearless composure of the young disciple disarmed his resentment, and forced him to exclaim, in astonishment, ' What greegree do you wear, that you dare do these things?' 'I wear no greegree,' was the beautiful reply, ' but I believe in the name of the Lord Jesus Christ.' Thus is Ethiopia sending forth her own sons ' to the help of the Lord against the mighty.' She is forging, within her own bosom, the weapons which are to annihilate her strong holds of ignorance and superstition.

"But it has been objected that the results of this Mission upon the mass, have not equalled the expectations of the Church—that they have not repaid the large expenditure of life and of treasure. It is true, that but few adults, *unconnected with the Mission*, have openly embraced the Gospel ; yet, even here, we are not without encouragement. The lever of divine truth, with quiet, but resistless energy, is gradually undermining the foundations of error. The faith of many, in their superstitions, is evidently shaken ; they cling less fondly to their idolatries, and thus the way is gradually preparing for the ultimate and yet more glorious triumphs of the Cross. * * * * * * * * * * *

"But disease and death have done their work in the African Mission, and it has been questioned ' whether this horrible waste of human life is longer necessary.' I may here remark, that the proportion of deaths in our own Mission has been remarkably small. Compared with similar institutions on the coast, ours has been eminently prosperous. The whole number of whites employed since its establishment is twenty. Of these six only have died, and two from diseases not attributable to the climate. * * * * * * * * * *

"Will not the Church furnish the men and the means for the more vigorous prosecution of this work ? We repeat that encouragement is not wanting. Already, a sunbeam here and there, hath brightened the prospect—and lo ! the horizon gleams with one streak, at least, of unclouded promise. ' Ethiopia shall stretch forth her hands unto God.' The day advances ; and, though it may not reach its meridian height before ' the glorious appearing of our Lord and Saviour Jesus Christ,' will it not be a blessed privilege, to have scattered one cloud of error and helped to prepare the way of our God !''

THE END.

APPENDIX.

PERHAPS nothing has so much retarded the Missionary work in Africa, as the opinion, generally entertained, of the effect of the climate upon the European constitution. This is regarded by many as so inevitably fatal, as to oppose an insuperable barrier to the labors of the white man in that extensive field. Although the subject has been incidentally noticed in the foregoing pages, the writer deems its importance a sufficient apology for introducing the following testimony from sources entitled to the highest respect

In his journal of January, 1846, Dr. Savage remarks, that since his arrival, nine years before, the whole number of laborers employed by different denominations had been sixty-one; and continues: "The whole number that have died is twenty, seven females and thirteen males; four of whom were from south, and fourteen from north of the Potomac; two were natives of England. The deaths in the case of the males are nearly two to one of females, contradicting the frequent declaration that the climate is more fatal to the constitution or system of the latter than to that of the former. Nothing particular need be said respecting the causes and circumstances operating in the cases of those who have died. This may be stated, that several cases might be mentioned, in which other influences might be assigned than those of the climate as the direct cause of their death; the majority, however, were undoubtedly victims of a climate more or less unfavorable to all foreign systems. * * * *ₗThe truth is, that the whole West Coast of Africa is an unhealthful portion of the globe; and

whoever resides here must have the standard of health lowered
more or less in all cases. The native of West Africa has not the
same degree of health and strength as his brother of the same
complexion in temperate climes. If not the native, then surely
not the colonist, coming from more healthful parts of the United
States; which is found to be the case. I have never found but
two who would say that they had the same degree of strength
here as in America, and they, I know, cannot make the same
declaration, with truth, now. There are many diseases, and much
death from disease among the native population, as well as among
other classes of residents in West Africa. But this does not
prove that the white man cannot live here. He has, does, and
can live for years, and is accomplishing a great work for futurity;
a work that will be equal to thirty, forty, and fifty years of human
life in other lands."

The following observations are extracted from an excellent
tract by the Rev. John Leighton Wilson, entitled, "The Agency
devolving on White men in Missions to Western Africa."

"The insalubrity of the climate has been, and I presume ever
will be, to a less or greater extent, a serious hindrance to the
progress of the gospel in Western Africa; and this difficulty
exists, be it known, irrespective of the kind of agency that may
be employed in carrying it on. For the colored man from the
United States is as sure to feel the effects of the climate, as the
white man; and if the physical constitution of the former possesses
some advantage in adapting itself more readily to the climate, I
am not sure but the other will have equally as much advantage
in his superior discretion and the precautionary measures which
he will practice to preserve his health.

"The difficulty, however, in either case, has been unduly mag-
nified; and so far as it has had the practical effect to turn away
the attention of candidates for the ministry from Africa, it has
had the tendency, not only to unsettle their own moral courage,
but greatly to aggravate the wrongs of an oppressed and injured
people.

"I have remarked, that the unhealthiness of the climate has

been exaggerated, and have now to show the foundation upon which this opinion rests.

"The Christian public in this country has had no means of forming a judgment on the subject, except by the number of deaths that have occurred among their missionaries; and these have been paraded before the public mind by the opposers of African missions with such studied care, that no one case has failed to produce its full effect.

"Now whilst no one can be more sensible than ourselves of the extent and severity of these losses, we feel that it has been specially unfortunate for the cause of truth and humanity, that the attendant circumstances and collateral causes of most of these calamities, have not been made equally prominent at the same time.

"And first, there are certain points along the coast of Africa, as in all other countries, that, by local causes, have been rendered more unhealthy than the country generally. Of these, none are supposed to be more so, than Sierra Leone and Cape Mesurado. I do not remember ever to have heard a dissent from this opinion by a single individual, whose judgment was entitled to respect; and yet it is from statistics of sickness and mortality that have occurred at these two places chiefly, that the public, both in England and America, have derived their impressions of the unhealthiness of the country at large.

"But there are other and still weightier considerations.

"I allude to the peculiar difficulties and trials, in which most of the missions to Africa have had their origin.

"It will be borne in mind, that all of them, except those of Sierra Leone and Gambia, have been founded within the last fifteen years. The places selected for most of these were not only on new and unbroken ground, so far as all missionary influence was concerned, but many of them were located in the bosom of heathen tribes who had enjoyed scarcely any intercourse with the civilized world. Most of the missionaries were pioneers in a difficult undertaking. They were unfurnished with missionary experience, and in many instances they were without the aid of

Christian counsel. They found themselves, at the commencement
of their labors, among a people who could not comprehend the
object of their mission, and who regarded all their professions of
friendship and disinterestedness with distrust. They were ignorant of the native character, and it required much labor to
master their barbarous languages, through which alone they
could arrive at correct knowledge of their character, or hope to
influence their minds. In many instances, they were without
medical aid, and in others, when physicians were at hand, those
physicians themselves were inexperienced in the treatment of
African diseases; and in every case, the missionaries were pressed
down by the cares, anxieties and responsibilities incident to all
new missions. So that when all these things are taken into
the account, we almost wonder that the mortality has not been
greater; we almost marvel that any have escaped.

" But this perilous crisis, we believe, has been passed. The
most formidable obstacles have been removed, and the missionary
work, it is believed, will henceforth move forward more easily
and with less sacrifice of life. Missionaries in that country, notwithstanding their losses, their reverses, their afflictions and
bereavements; have been sustained in their work, and obtained a
firm footing on many points along that coast. A large amount
of missionary experience has been acquired; the roughness of
native character has been smoothed down; the habits, customs,
and feelings of the natives are better understood by the missionaries, and the objects of the missionaries are better understood by
the natives. Many of the most difficult dialects of the country
have been reduced to writing, and now serve, not only as easy
and direct channels of conveying religious truth to the minds of
the people, but will serve as a clue to the acquisition of all other
languages in the country. Missionaries going to that country
hereafter, will find missionary brethren on the ground to welcome
them and give them all needed counsel and aid. In this way
they will escape much of the wasting care and anxieties that
were unavoidable at the commencement of this undertaking.
They may now go to that country with the reasonable prospect

of living, and if they cannot calculate upon enjoying the same amount of vigorous and elastic health, that they would in their native country, they may at least expect to have strength enough to proclaim the unsearchable riches of the gospel to thousands of their fellow men, who are perishing for the want of it. There is a reasonable prospect that white missionaries, provided they are endowed with the faith, the courage and the perseverance befitting their high calling, may live in that country to establish Christian churches there, which will be able, in due time, not only to sustain themselves, but to communicate their blessings to the remotest regions of that benighted continent.

" But it has been affirmed and re-affirmed, that white men cannot live in that country. And who are they that maintain this opinion so confidently ? Men of the world ? No ! *They* live there, and labor there, and make money there, notwithstanding all this outcry about the unhealthiness of the country.

" Without pretending to give precise statistics, we presume that we are strictly in the bounds of truth, when we say that the number of whites residing on that coast, and on islands adjacent to that coast, cannot be less than three thousand. If we add to this the floating population, engaged in commerce and in the suppression of the slave-trade, the whole population cannot be less than eight or ten thousand.

' In spite of the reputed unhealthiness of the country, European governments can find officers to govern their civil establishments, and soldiers to garrison their fortifications. Merchants in Europe and America can find men, not only to sail their vessels in those seas, but they have their agents on shore—aye ! and as many of them as they wish—to gather around them the rich products of the country. Science, too, finds no difficulty in getting agents to carry on her researches in those regions. And we may add to all this, that there is a considerable number of individuals of affluence, who reside in that country as a matter of preference.

" But what is the missionary corps among all these ? They do not form the one-hundredth part of the whole. And what is the inference ? What is the verdict that posterity will pronounce upon this strange fact? It can be nothing else than that motives of gain and worldly ambition are a hundred fold more powerful, in the present age, than all the zeal and love of the Christian churches of the same period.

"Let us pursue this humiliating comparison a step further.

"The number of Protestant missionaries residing on the coast of Africa has never, at any period, been half so great as that of those who have resided there for the purpose of carrying on the slave-trade. Here then is a class of men, who, in opposition to every dictate of conscience and humanity; in defiance of all the great powers of the earth; in the midst of cares, perplexities, and disappointments that seldom fall to the lot of any other set of men ;—find it practicable to live in that country, and not only so, but at the most insalubrious points, and among the most savage tribes on the coast. And can any inference be drawn from this fact that shall not fasten reproach upon the followers of the Saviour? Are we willing that history shall record the fact, that ungodly men live in Africa, to degrade and ruin her sons and daughters, but that we cannot live there to rescue them from everlasting destruction.

" We have little or no hesitation in saying, that if the Church of Christ had, during the two last centuries, made one half the effort to christianize Africa, that men of the world have to degrade and to ruin her, long ere this that entire continent, instead of being proverbial as it now is for ignorance and idolatry, would have been filled with the light and the blessings of the gospel. And we have as little hesitation in predicting, that, if the churches will henceforth make efforts somewhat commensurate with those that are likely to be made by the world to draw out her commercial resources, the present century shall not pass away before Africa, yes, miserable, degraded Africa, shall be brought under the power and the dominion of the gospel. Faith and courage and patient perseverance, under the guidance of the Holy Ghost, will assuredly triumph over every difficulty, be it imaginary, or be it real.